Bob Timberlake

Cover: The Studio, 1974 (cat. no. 26)

Copyright © 1979 by the North Carolina Museum of Art, Raleigh, North Carolina 27611.
All rights reserved. Printed in the United States of America.

Library of Congress Cataloging in publication data

Timberlake, Bob.
  The art of Bob Timberlake.

  1. Timberlake, Bob—Exhibitions. I. North
Carolina. Museum of Art, Raleigh. II. Title.
ND237.T556A4   1979   759.13   79-19629
ISBN 0-88259-094-4

 North Carolina Department of Cultural Resources

The Art of Bob Timberlake

September 16 - October 14, 1979

North Carolina Museum of Art, Raleigh

Lenders to the Exhibition

Mrs. Harry V. Anderson, Jr.
Mr. and Mrs. John A. Carter
Mr. and Mrs. Frank E. Driscoll
Dr. and Mrs. C. Richard Epes
Federal Reserve Bank of Richmond
Mr. and Mrs. Daniel M. Galbreath
Mr. and Mrs. Robert L. Grubb
Mr. and Mrs. Douglas E. Ix
Dr. and Mrs. Joseph M. Jacobson
Mr. and Mrs. David E. Maas
The R. W. Norton Art Gallery

Mr. and Mrs. K. G. Phillips
Mrs. Marlot H. Phillips
Dr. and Mrs. David A. Roberts
Mr. and Mrs. Eddie Smith, Sr.
Mr. and Mrs. J. Harold Smith
Mr. and Mrs. Robert L. Smith
Mr. and Mrs. Bob Timberlake
Mr. and Mrs. C. H. Timberlake, Sr.
Mrs. Kay M. Timberlake
Lynn Foushee Timberlake
Jane and Jimmy Townsend

Acknowledgments

It is rare that an artist would achieve fame and wide popularity in such a short span of time as has Bob Timberlake. Since he became active as a painter over the past nine years, Mr. Timberlake has become one of North Carolina's favorite artists. His first one-man show was in his native state in 1970 at the Southeastern Center for Contemporary Art in Winston-Salem. In 1973 he was given a one-man show at Hammer Galleries in New York City. It was a sellout, as were all his subsequent exhibitions at the same gallery. His multiple reproduction editions have spread his reputation throughout the country and abroad. The present exhibition is part of the Museum's program of recognizing artists of North Carolina who have achieved certain levels of accomplishment in their respective fields.

In acknowledging the efforts of those who organized the exhibition and prepared the catalogue, one of course must begin by thanking the artist, who not only has lent a number of works to the show but has also given generously of his time throughout its planning stages, as did his associates Hugh Morton, Jr., Frank Stoner, Collette Childers, and Shirley Lohr. Dorothy B. Rennie, the exhibition's organizer, is to be commended for her essay on the artist as well as for her able handling of the numerous details of assembling the show. On behalf of the Art Commission and the North Carolina Department of Cultural Resources, I would like to acknowledge our debt to the lenders, without whose cooperation the exhibition would not have been realized.

Moussa M. Domit, Director

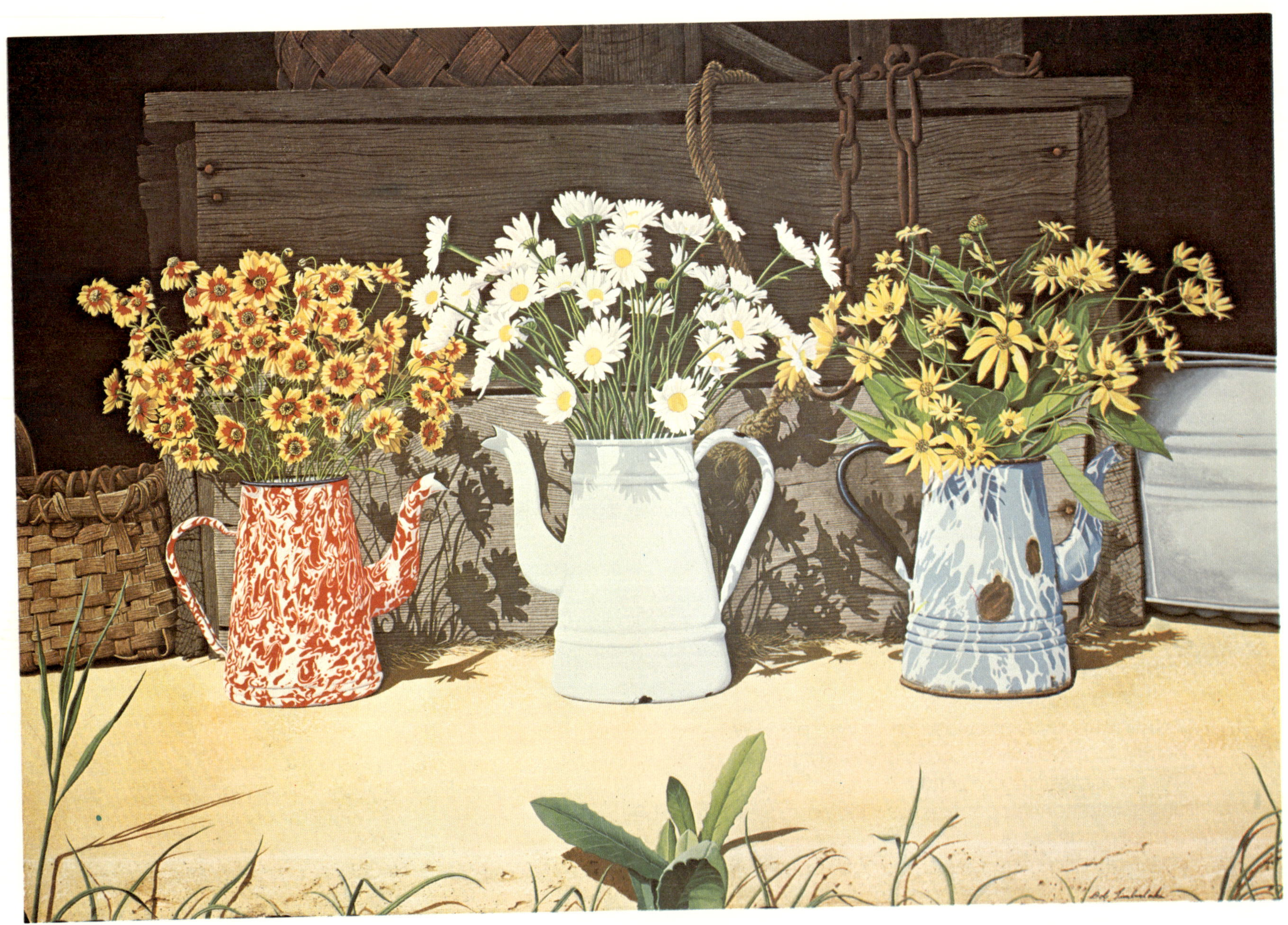

Daisies 1978 (cat. no. 43)

Introduction

The success story of Bob Timberlake as an artist has acquired an almost mythical quality in less than a decade. He did not plan to be an artist, although he began to draw at age eight and at fifteen won the National Industrial Arts Award, sponsored by Ford Motor Company, for a Pennsylvania Dutch dowry chest which he designed, built, and decorated (cat. no. 1). Painting was a hobby for most of his life until a fateful day in 1969 when he drove up to Chadds Ford, Pennsylvania, for a visit with Andrew Wyeth and his wife. Before this visit Timberlake had been moved by a layout on Andrew Wyeth and his work in **Life** magazine and had begun to work seriously for control in his own painting during his spare time. When he could paint a leaf to look as real as the real thing, he felt that perhaps he had gained control of his medium; but he was still not very objective about his painting and felt that he needed an established artist to tell him whether he had any talent—enough to pursue an art career.

Previous circumstances had led him to a meeting with Dr. Margaret Handy, a pioneer doctor in the Chadds Ford area, who had been pediatrician to the Wyeth children. Timberlake discussed his dilemma with Dr. Handy, and she urged him to call Andrew Wyeth, who very obligingly agreed to look at his paintings. After encouraging words from Wyeth, Bob Timberlake's resolve to paint grew daily, until he finally gave up his responsibilities in five family businesses, bought a two-hundred-year-old house for his studio, and took up his brushes to paint in earnest in 1970. Since that time, almost every morning his station wagon has traveled the back roads from Lexington to **Another World** (cat. no. 28).

While an artist's studio is his private domain, Bob Timberlake's studio is not just a "hideaway." It is a place where he works hard and finds inspiration. His art has been largely self-motivated and self-developed, since he has had no formal art training; and it has taken many laborious hours of trial and error to master his technique. He works with watercolor and tempera, media which can be altered, but which require a great amount of control on the artist's part. Timberlake says that he usually has a painting finished in his own mind before he begins to paint. He works from nature, and unlike many artists of today, sometimes makes several detailed pencil studies of a subject before he takes brush in hand.

Just as Andrew Wyeth has found all the scope necessary for his art in the area of Brandywine Valley and Chadds Ford, so Bob Timberlake has found his world of creativity in a limited area of North Carolina—in the Piedmont section, in and around Lexington where he now lives, and Salisbury, where he was born and grew up. He wandered through the fields and woods of this area during his boyhood and developed a keen and observant eye for nature at an early age. He has stated that he could spend months at his cabin studio—never stepping off the front porch— and never run out of subjects to paint.

Timberlake chooses subject matter which expresses simple pleasures and moods of nostalgia—old houses with rusty rooftops, gnarled trees on country roads, harvest fruit in baskets, and pots of flowers on a window sill. He paints the plain and ordinary without glorifying or vilifying his subject. While there may be a story or the hint of a personality behind some of his paintings—for example, "Mrs. Leonard's Marigolds" or "Mr. Petrea's Chair"—his paintings are essentially unpeopled.

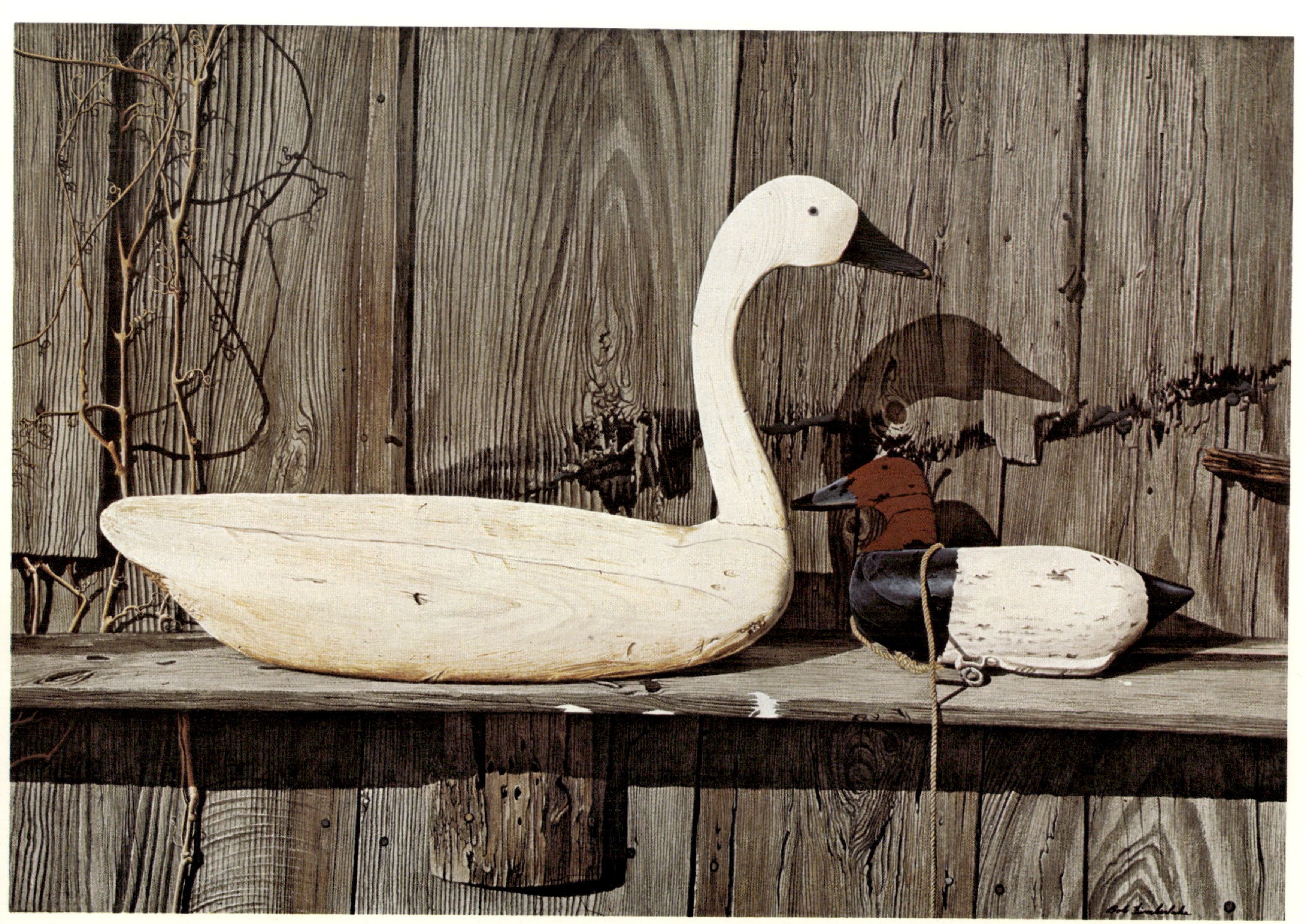
Knott's Island Decoys 1977 (cat. no. 39)

Bob Timberlake has been described as one of the three prominent regional artists in the American Realist School, sharing company with Eric Sloane of New England and Andrew Wyeth of Pennsylvania. However, it is quite apparent that Timberlake's paintings are outside the movement of "New Realism" or "Super Realism," which still appears to be at high tide in this country. His works are more prosaic, less obviously painterly, and contain not a twinge of eccentricity. In fact, about all that he has in common with the New Realists of today is his use of the camera when he wants to record quickly changing light and atmospheric conditions.

His art is more related to previous forms of representational art in the American tradition. For example, his **Knott's Island Decoys** (cat. no. 39) has some of the trompe l'oeil effect of a finely detailed still life by the nineteenth-century painter, William Harnett. However, Timberlake has not achieved the textural and atmospheric qualities found in Harnett's work. Some of his early paintings have a touch of naivete, but his later works appear to have more structural maturity, especially those done in 1978 (cat. nos. 45, 47).

Perhaps the only artist who has influenced Bob Timberlake is his mentor, Andrew Wyeth. However, there is very little, if any, similarity in the styles of the two artists. While both paint prosaic scenes from their own region, they paint in a decidedly different manner. Wyeth's work sometimes has sinister overtones, while Timberlake's brand of realism is non-threatening, somewhat idyllic, and quite out of step with today's plastic world. Perhaps this accounts for his wide popular appeal with the public.

Timberlake has never regarded himself as one of the "angry young artists"; in fact, he does not appear to fit into any of the artist stereotypes. He has not starved in a garret—quite the contrary, he has had phenomenal success at selling his paintings. He has felt no need to run away to the South Seas, or any other exotic place. His own backyard is his Eden, and he is quite content to stay in it with his devoted wife, Kay, and their three teen-agers, Kelly, Ed, and Dan.

Roberts Edgar Timberlake has always been an achiever. Aside from his career as an artist, he has many other interests. He restores antique automobiles and old houses, carves and paints duck decoys, and has one of the largest antique quilt collections in the state.

In 1978 President Carter honored him as "Official Artist for Keep America Beautiful," for which **Daisies** (cat. no. 43) was commissioned as the theme painting; and in 1979, he received the North Carolina Public Service Award, an honor which recognized the artist's civic and church work in his own hometown, the state, and the nation.

During his short career as an artist, Timberlake's work has been featured in dozens of magazines and newspapers, including articles in **The Reader's Digest, Audubon, Today's Art,** and **Southwest Art. The Bob Timberlake Collection**, a handsome leather-bound book of his art, with prose by Charles Kuralt, was published in a limited edition in 1977. The artist has recently written **The World of Bob Timberlake**, which also includes a selection of his works and will be published in the fall of 1979.

With all his precocious achievements, the artist remains a sensitive and unassuming southern gentleman who has a great love for his native state and finds joy in painting its beauty for others to see.

Dorothy B. Rennie

Catalogue

Dimensions are in inches, height preceding width.

Grubb's Gazebo 1978 (cat. no. 45)

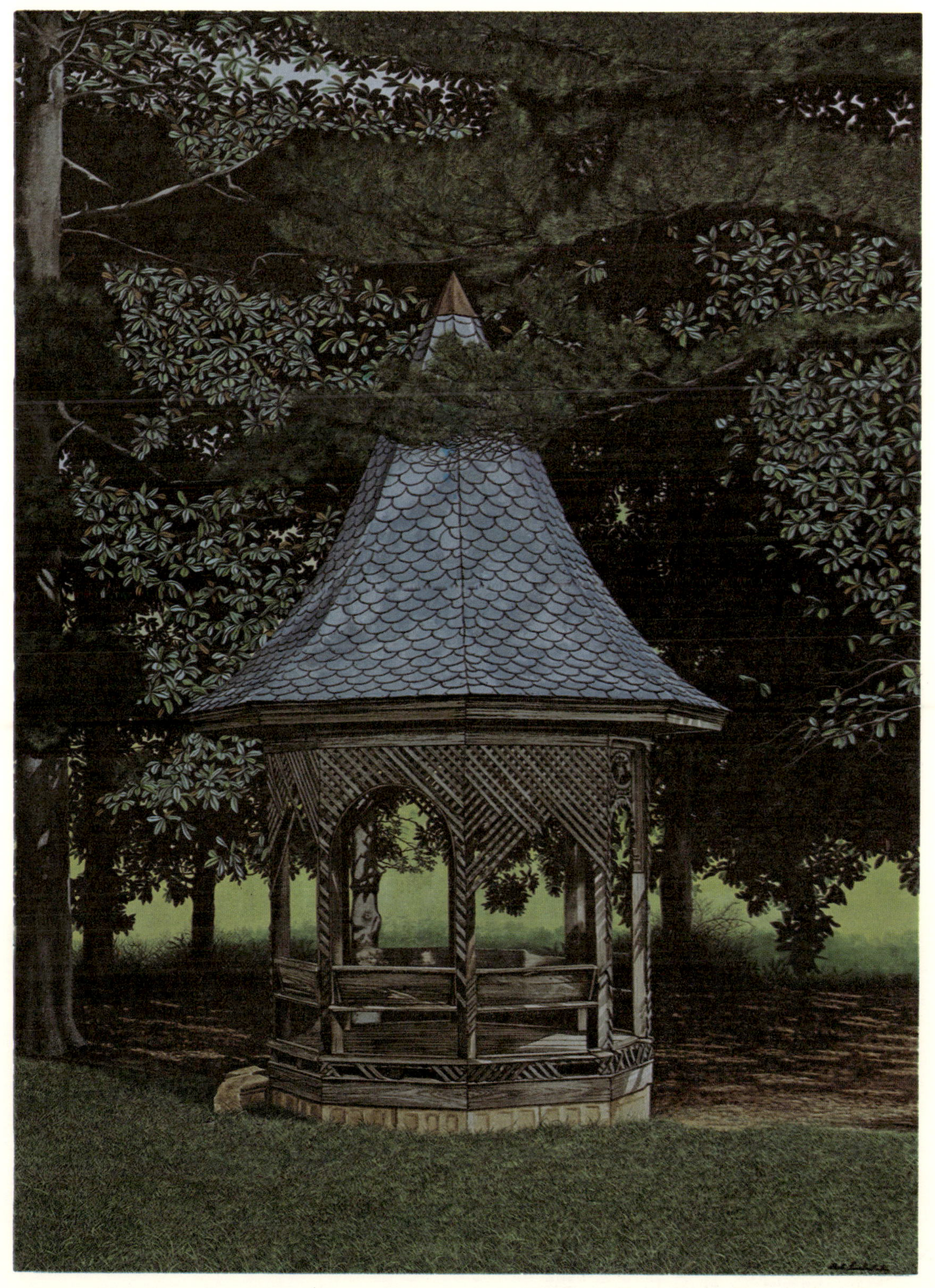

1. Pennsylvania Dutch Dowry Chest   1954
   Cedar and maple wood, lacquer   31 x 50½ x 26
   Lent by Mr. and Mrs. Bob Timberlake

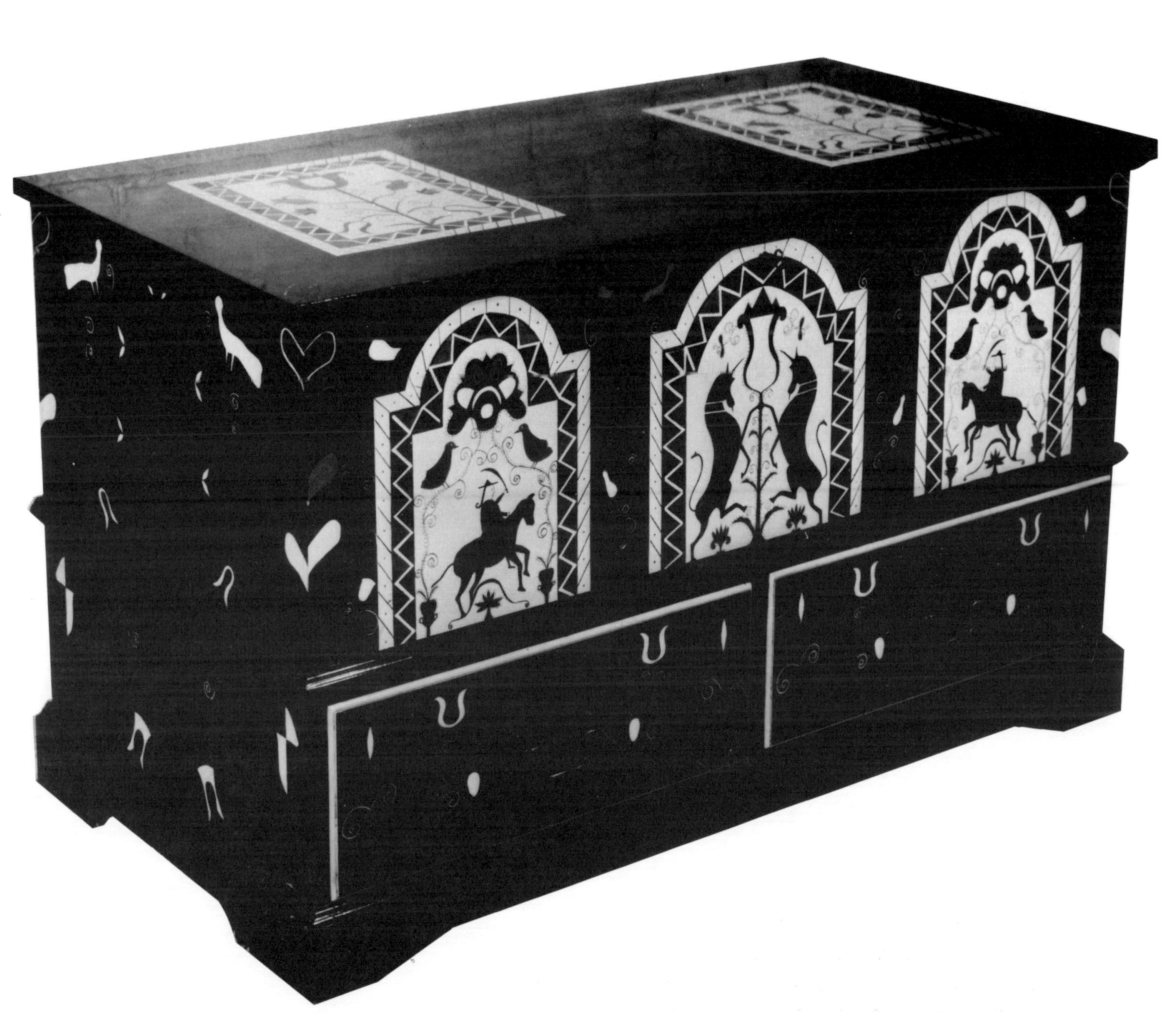

2. Old Feezor Place   1968
   Acrylic   (4) 8 x 10 paintings
   Inscribed lower right: Bob Timberlake
   Lent by Mr. and Mrs. Bob Timberlake

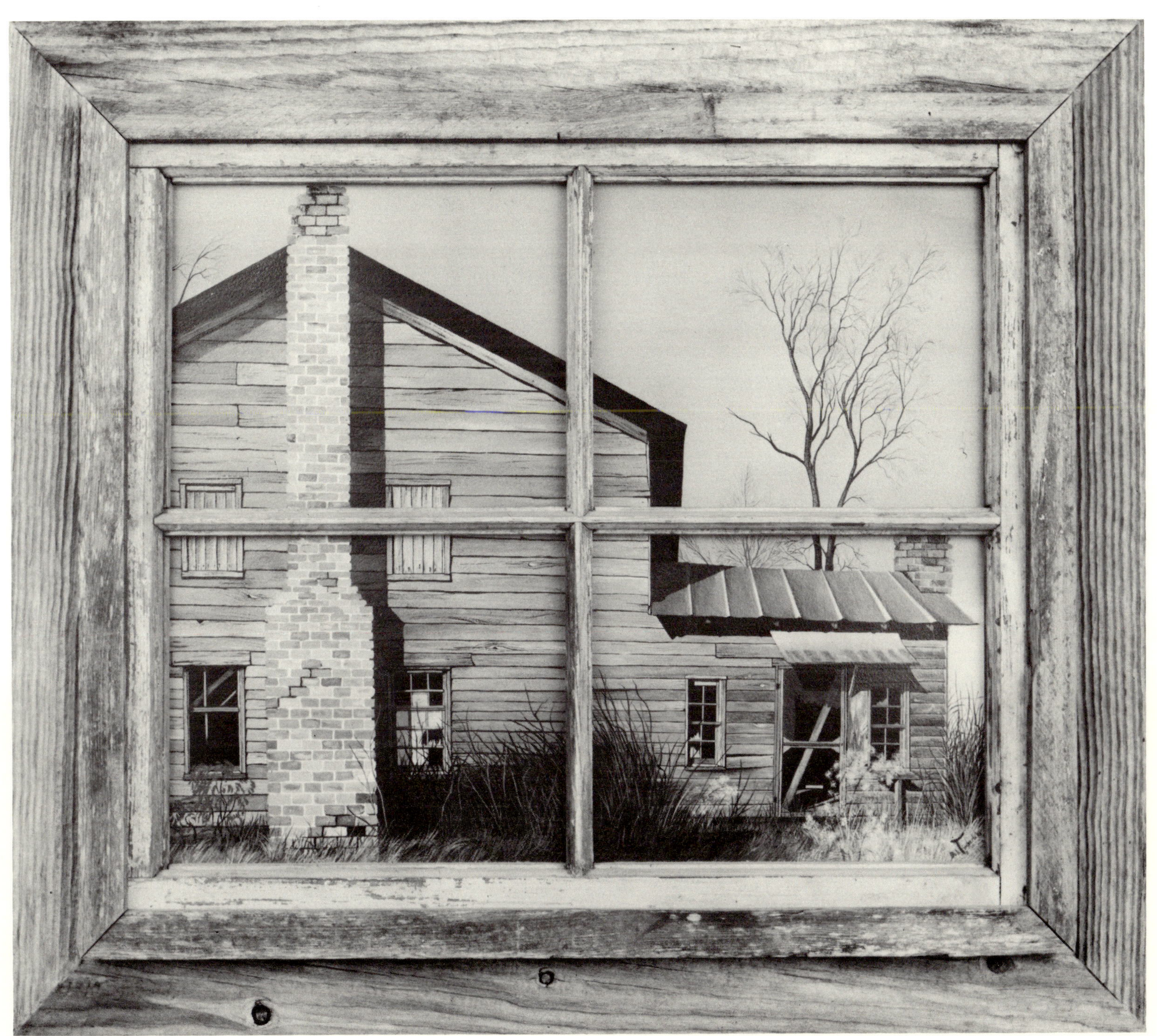

3. Study for June Cherries   1970
   Watercolor   14 x 21
   Inscribed lower right: Bob Timberlake
   Lent by Mrs. Kay M. Timberlake

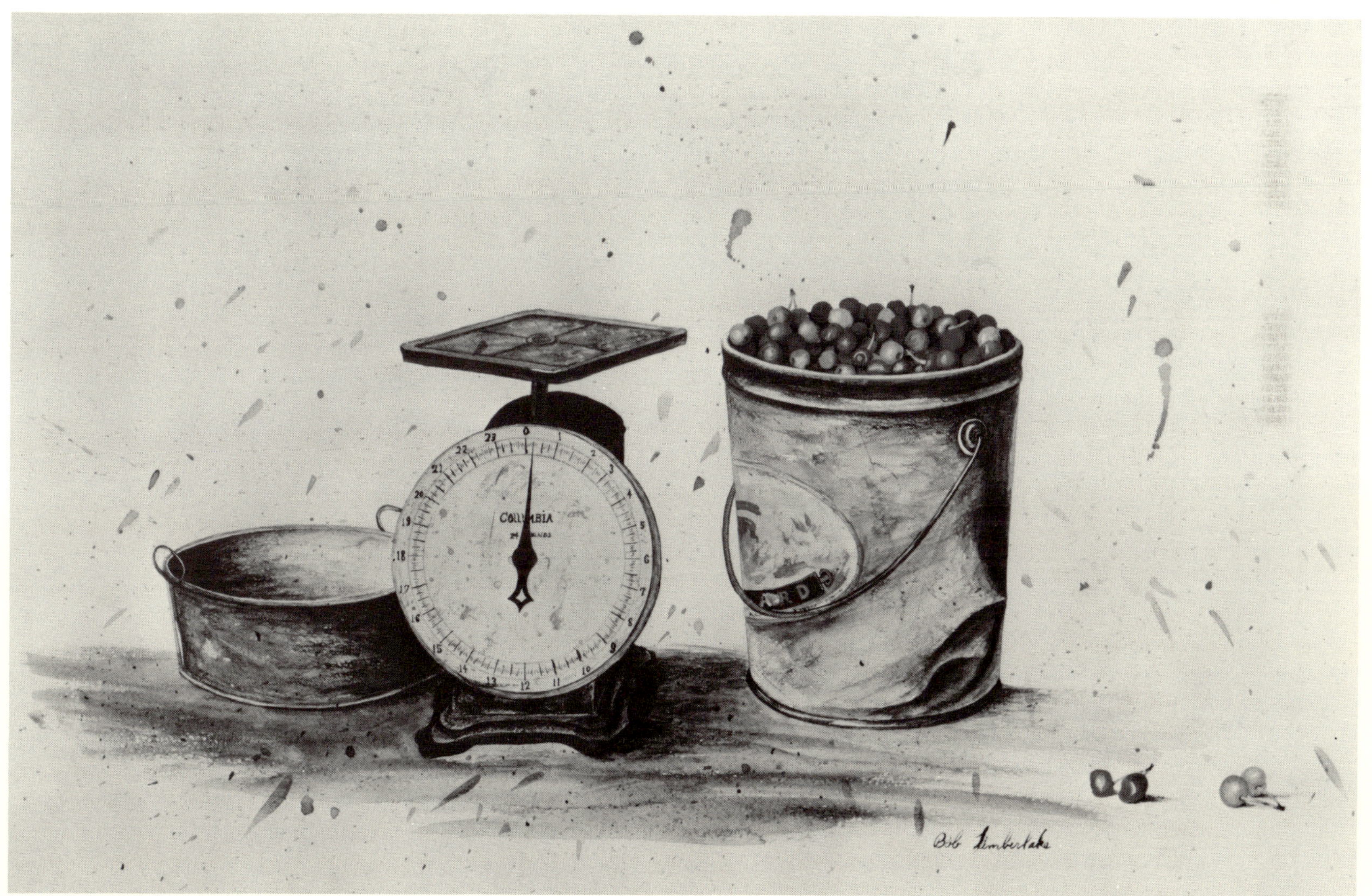

COLUMBIA
Bob Timberlake

4. June Cherries   1970
   Tempera   17 x 24
   Inscribed lower right: Bob Timberlake
   Private Collection

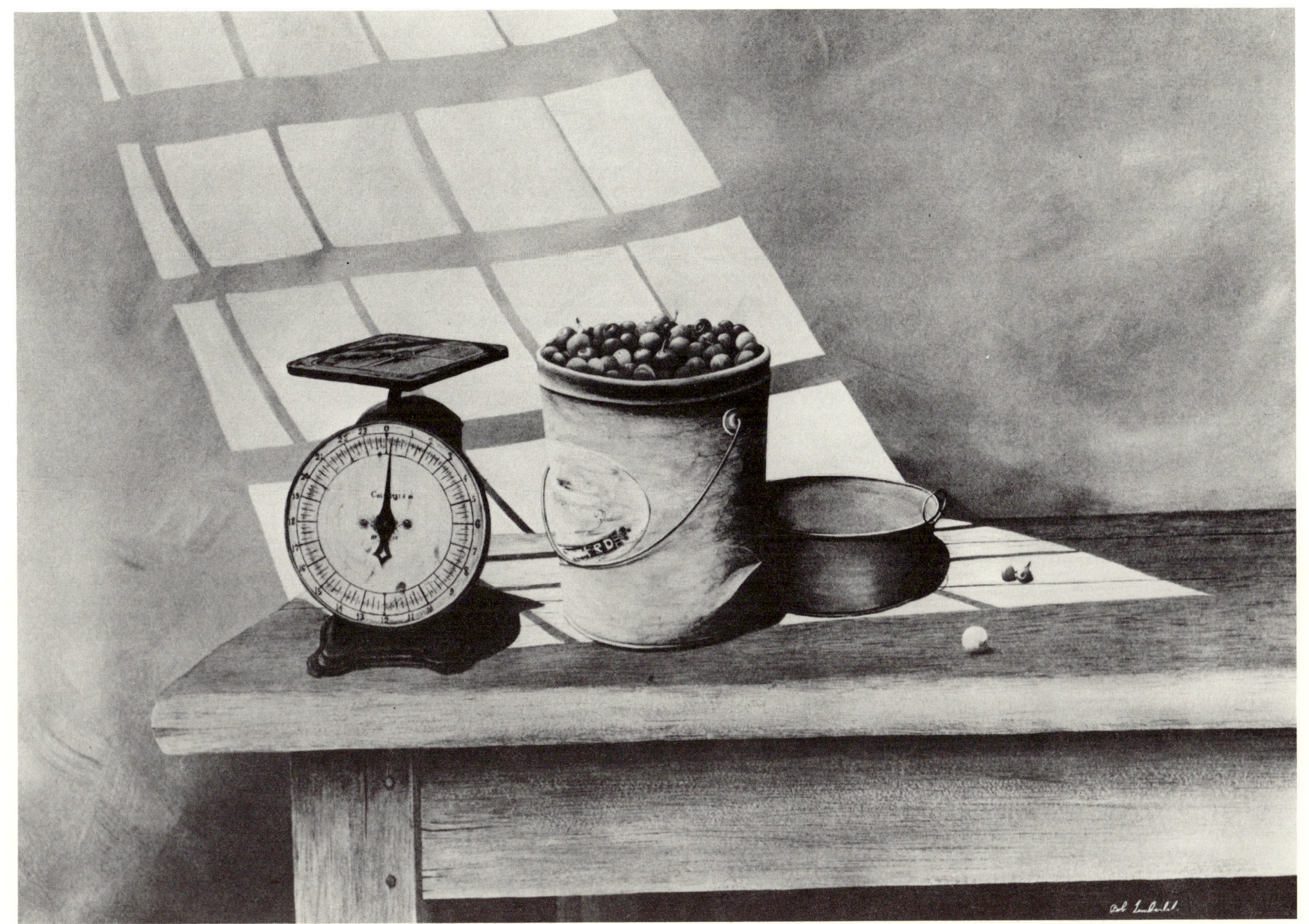

5. Ella's Cupboard   1970
   Tempera   18 x 24
   Inscribed lower right: Bob Timberlake
   Lent by Mr. and Mrs. C. H. Timberlake, Sr.

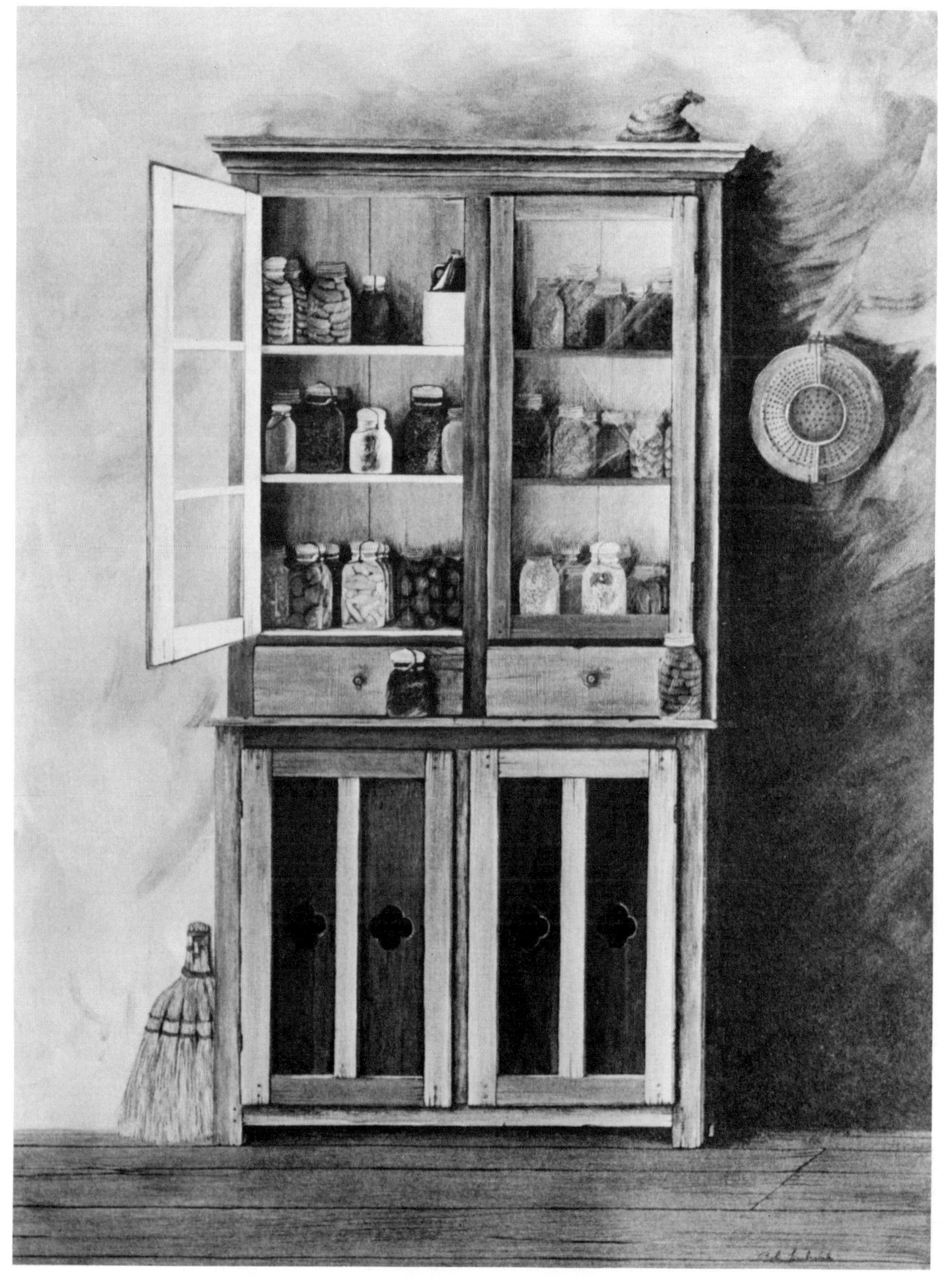

6. Study of Drum in Chair   1970
   Pencil   13½ x 11
   Inscribed lower center: Bob Timberlake
   Lent by Mr. and Mrs. J. Harold Smith

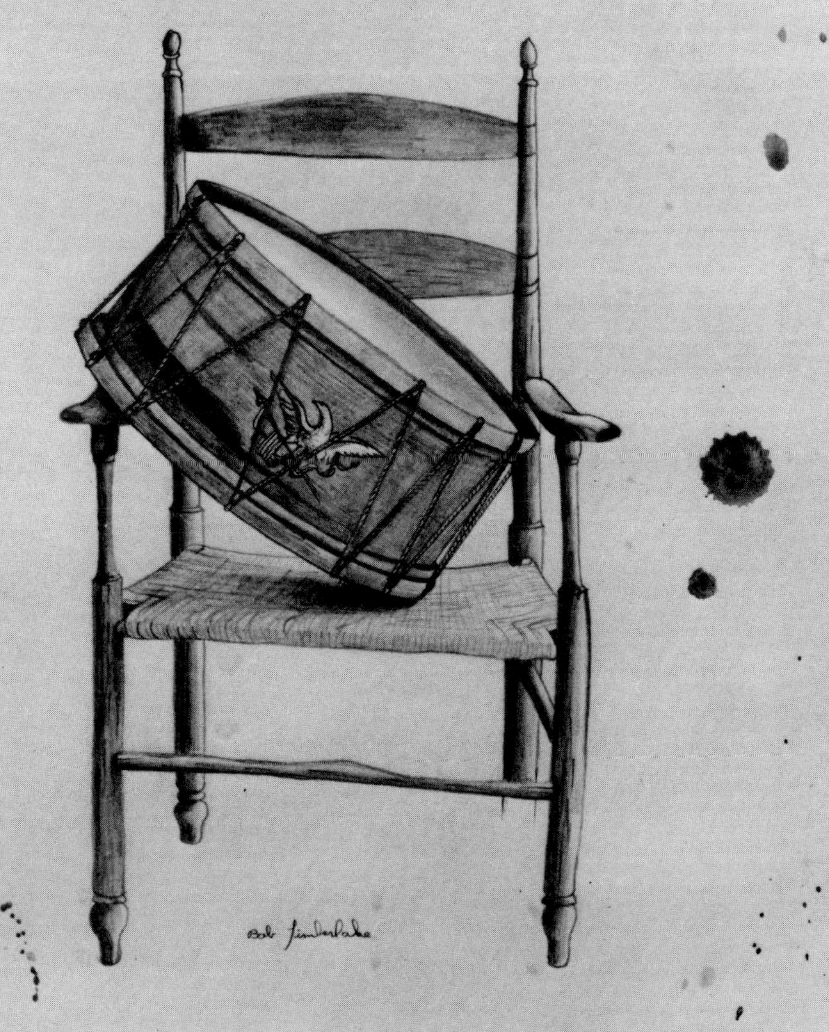

Bob Timberlake
Light from rt. back
A touch of sun or floor
at left front leg
↑
very bow-legged
front leg
Southern Windsor (arms come way out) and Yankee Drum

7. My Yankee Drum   1970
   Tempera   14 x 22
   Inscribed lower left: Bob Timberlake
   Lent by Mr. and Mrs. J. Harold Smith

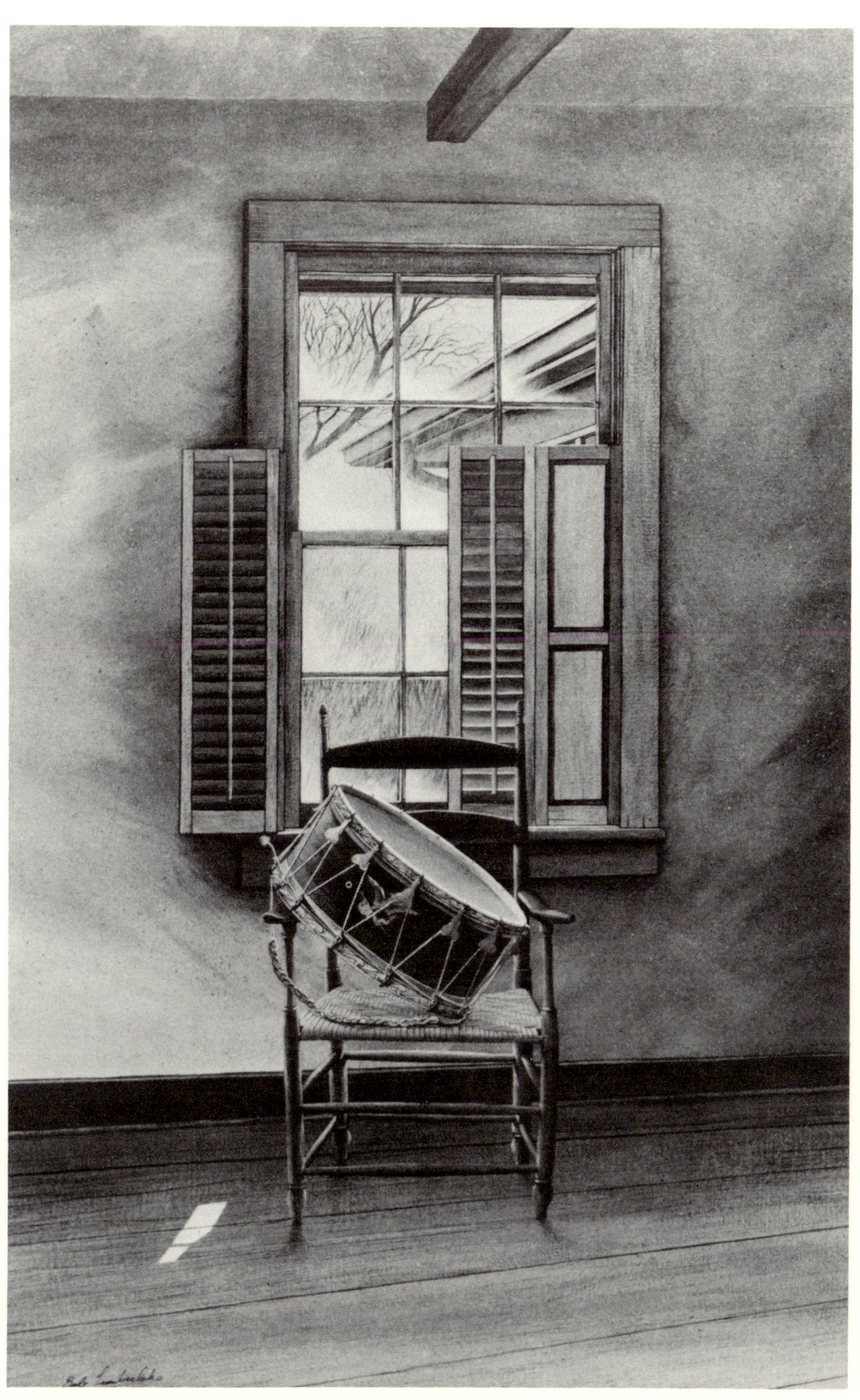

8. Mrs. Leonard's Marigolds   1972
   Watercolor   19 x 24¾
   Inscribed center right: Bob Timberlake
   Private Collection

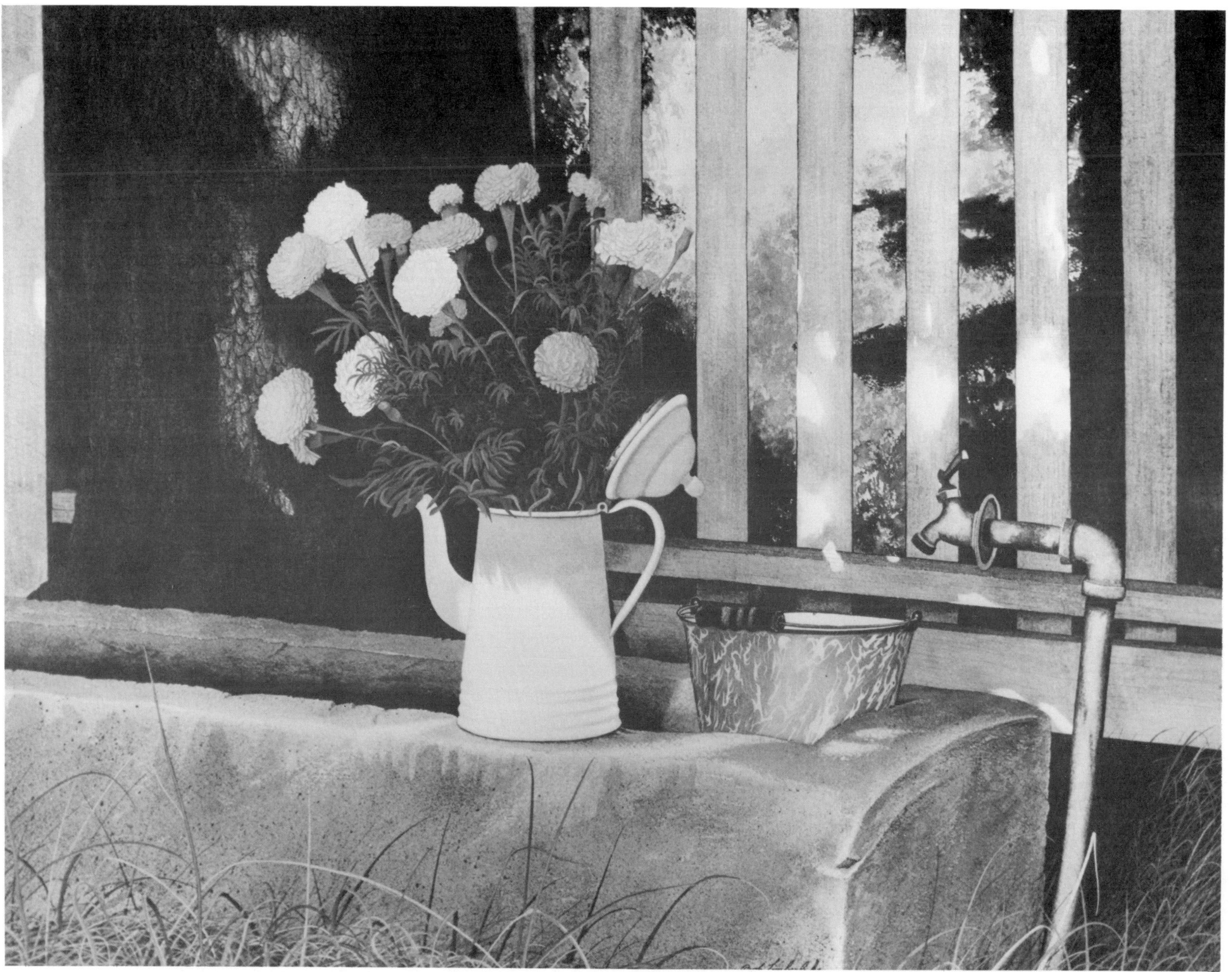

9. Cape Fear Lighthouse Site   1972
   Tempera   14½ x 30½
   Inscribed lower right: Bob Timberlake
   Lent by Mrs. Harry V. Anderson, Jr.

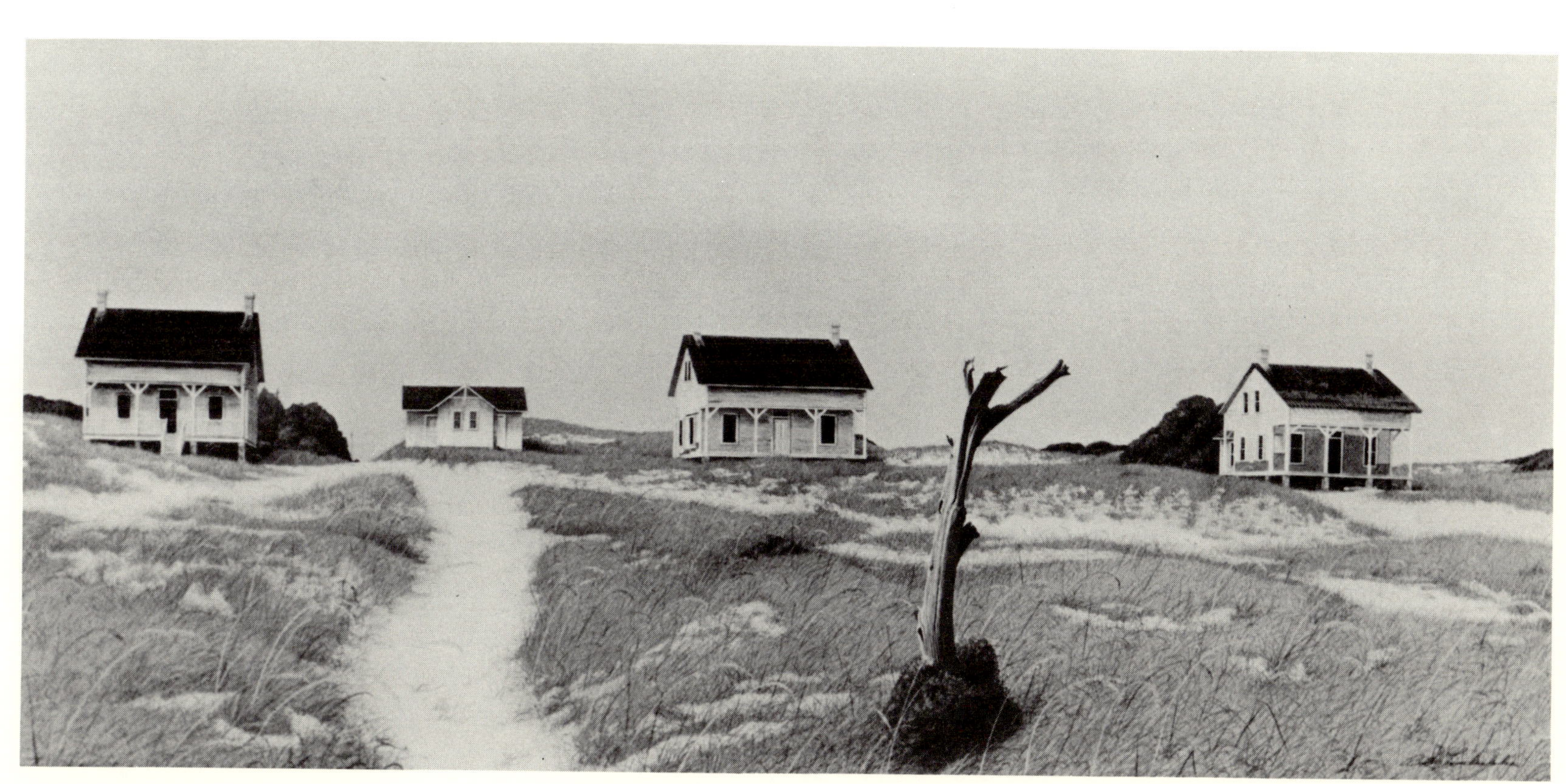

10. Rowboat   1972
    Tempera   18½ x 24½
    Inscribed lower right: Bob Timberlake
    Private Collection

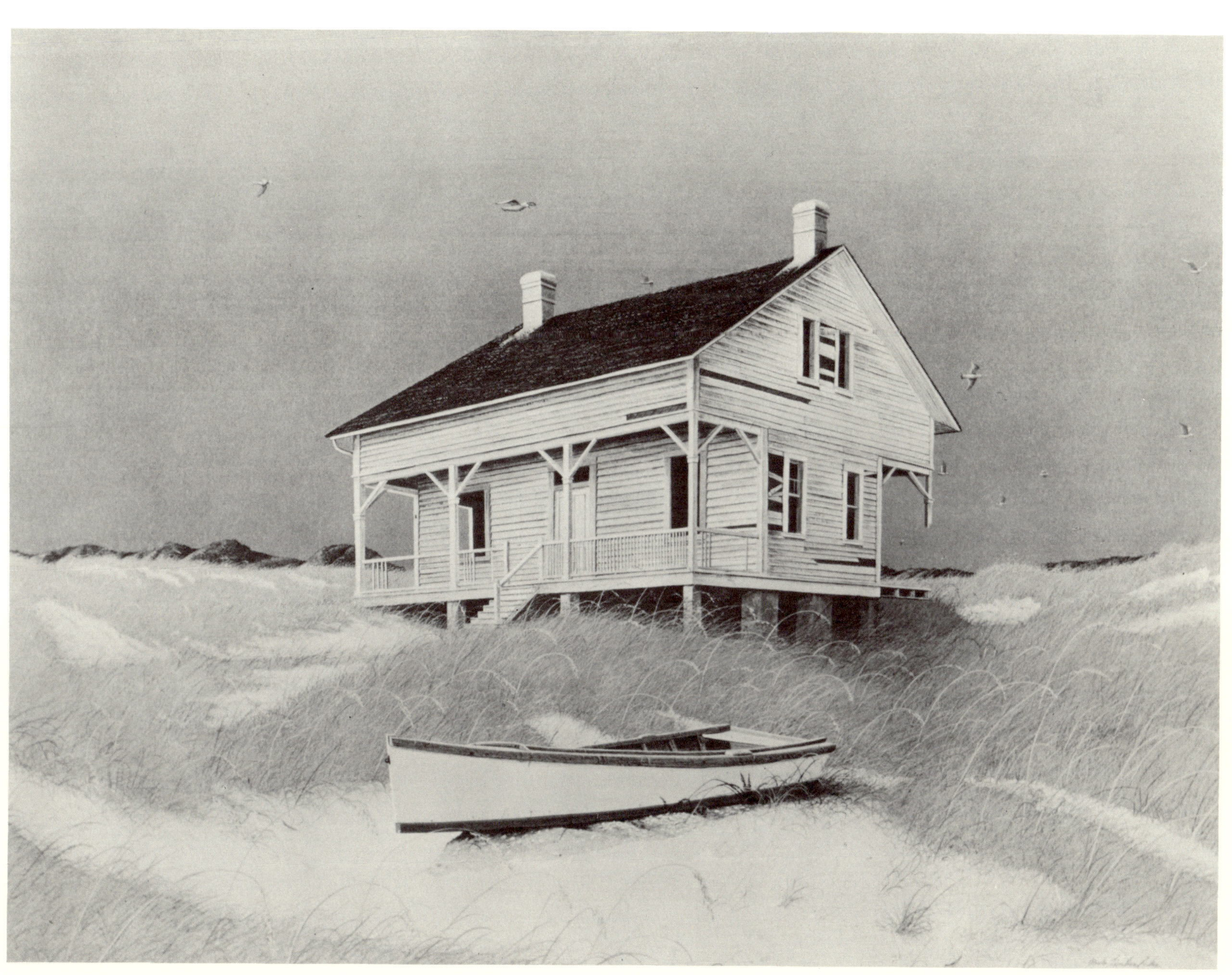

11. Bald Head Lighthouse   1972
    Tempera   19¼ x 15¼
    Inscribed lower right: Bob Timberlake
    Private Collection

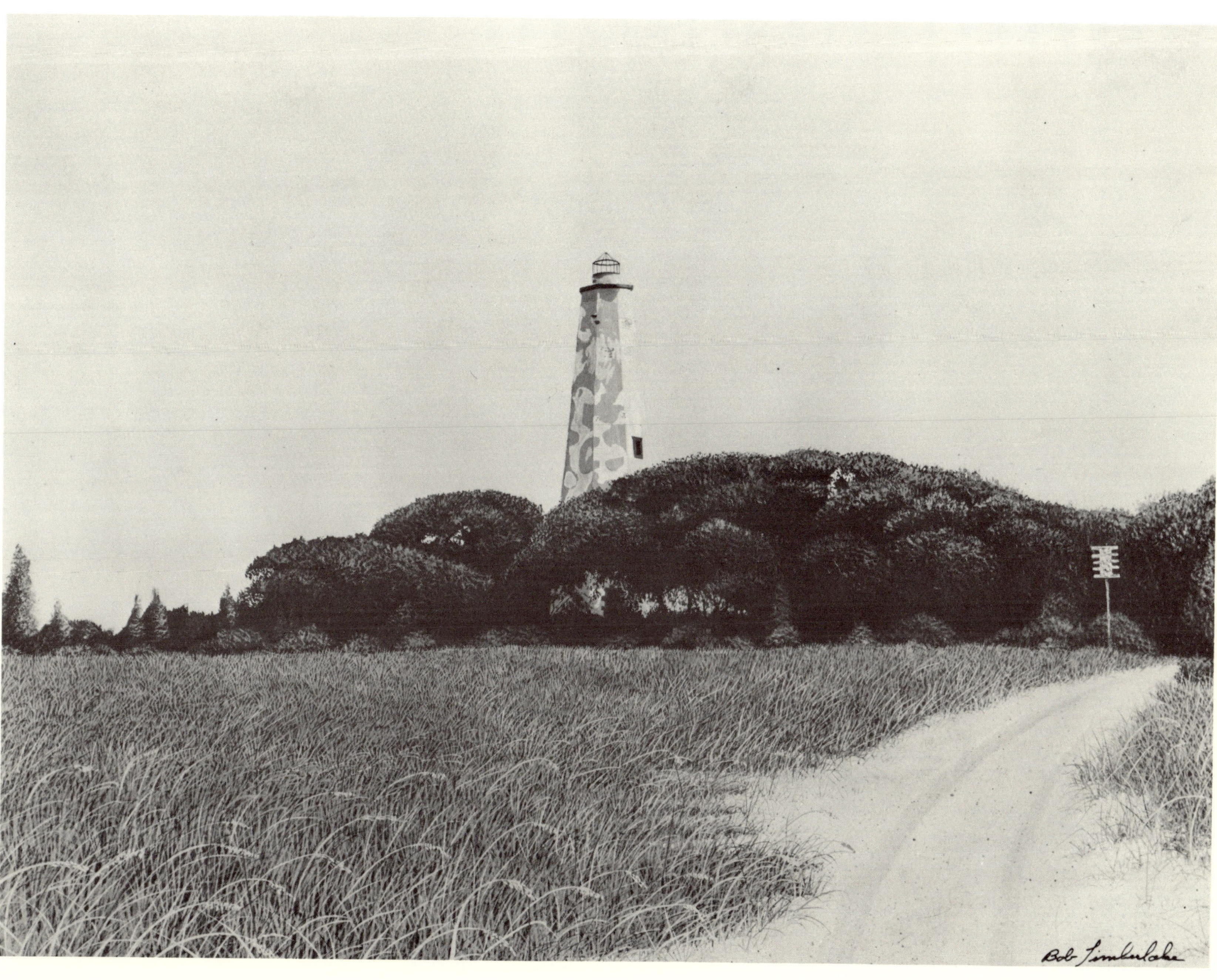

Bob Timberlake

12. Afternoon at The Petrea's   1972
    Watercolor   18¼ x 25½
    Inscribed lower right: Bob Timberlake
    Lent by Mr. and Mrs. K. G. Phillips

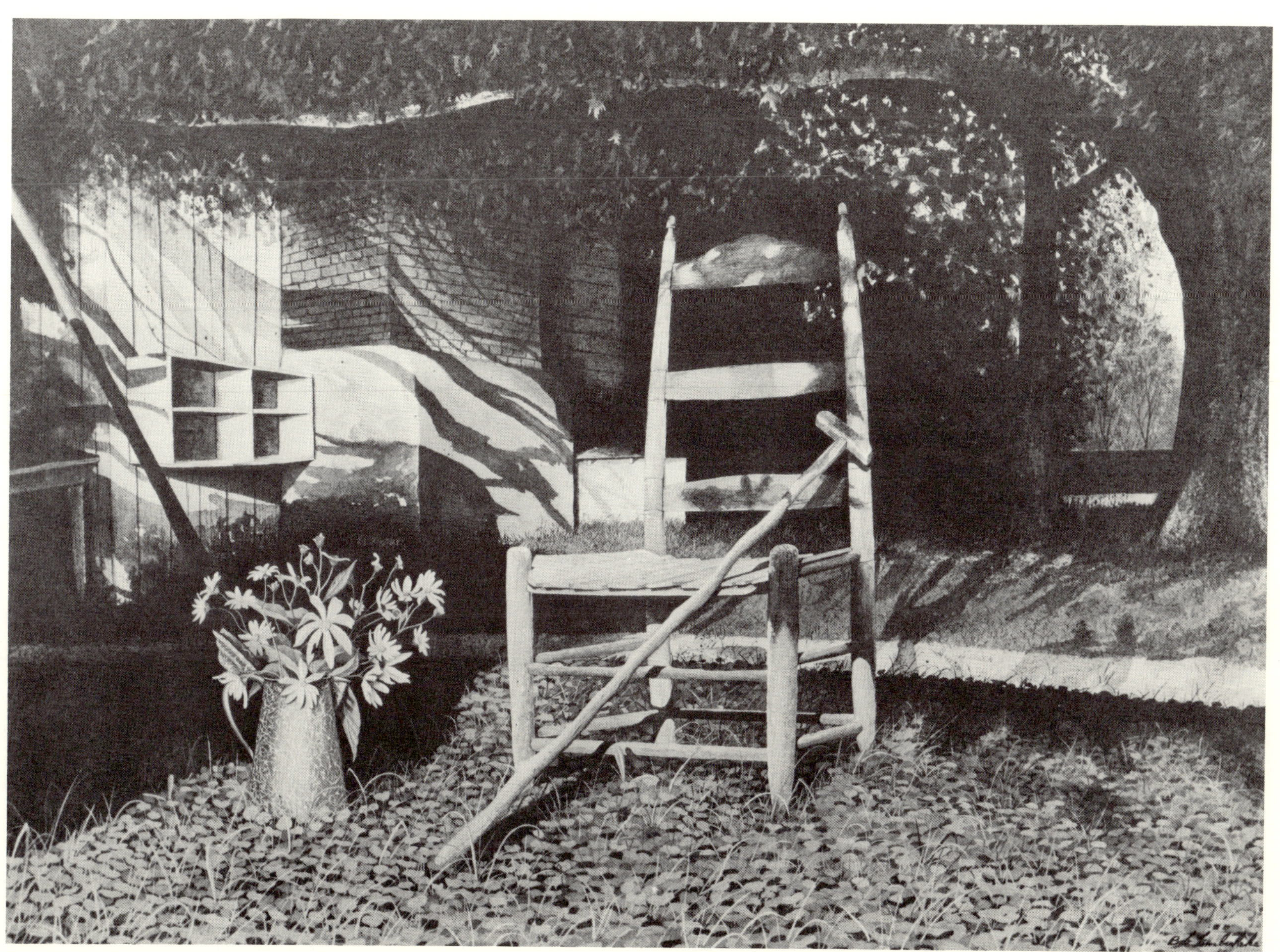

13. One Last Geranium   1972
    Watercolor   30 x 22¼
    Inscribed lower right: Bob Timberlake
    Lent by Mrs. Marlot H. Phillips

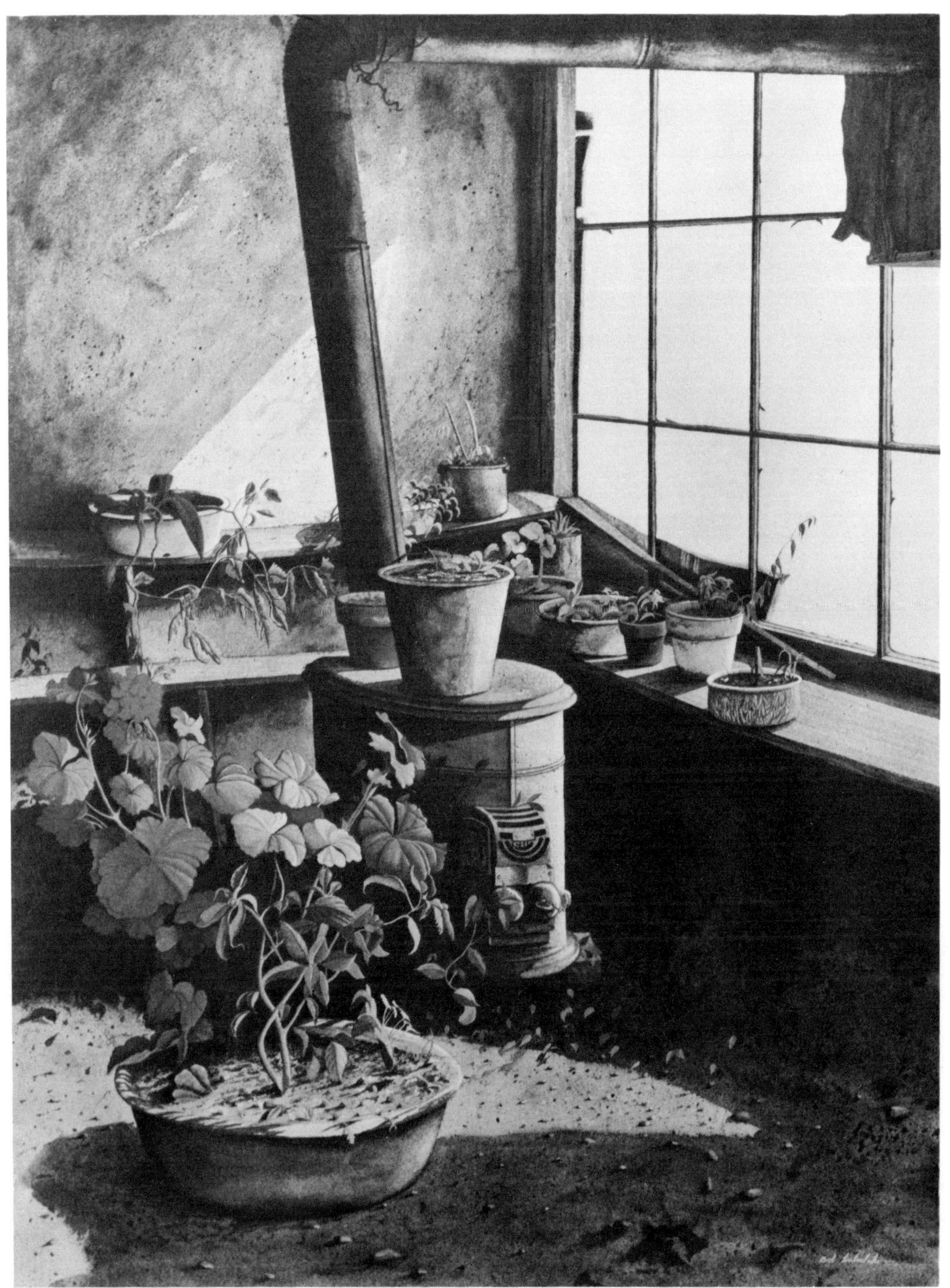

14. Mrs. Leonard's Backyard   1973
    Watercolor   22¼ x 30
    Inscribed lower right: Bob Timberlake
    Lent by Mr. and Mrs. John A. Carter

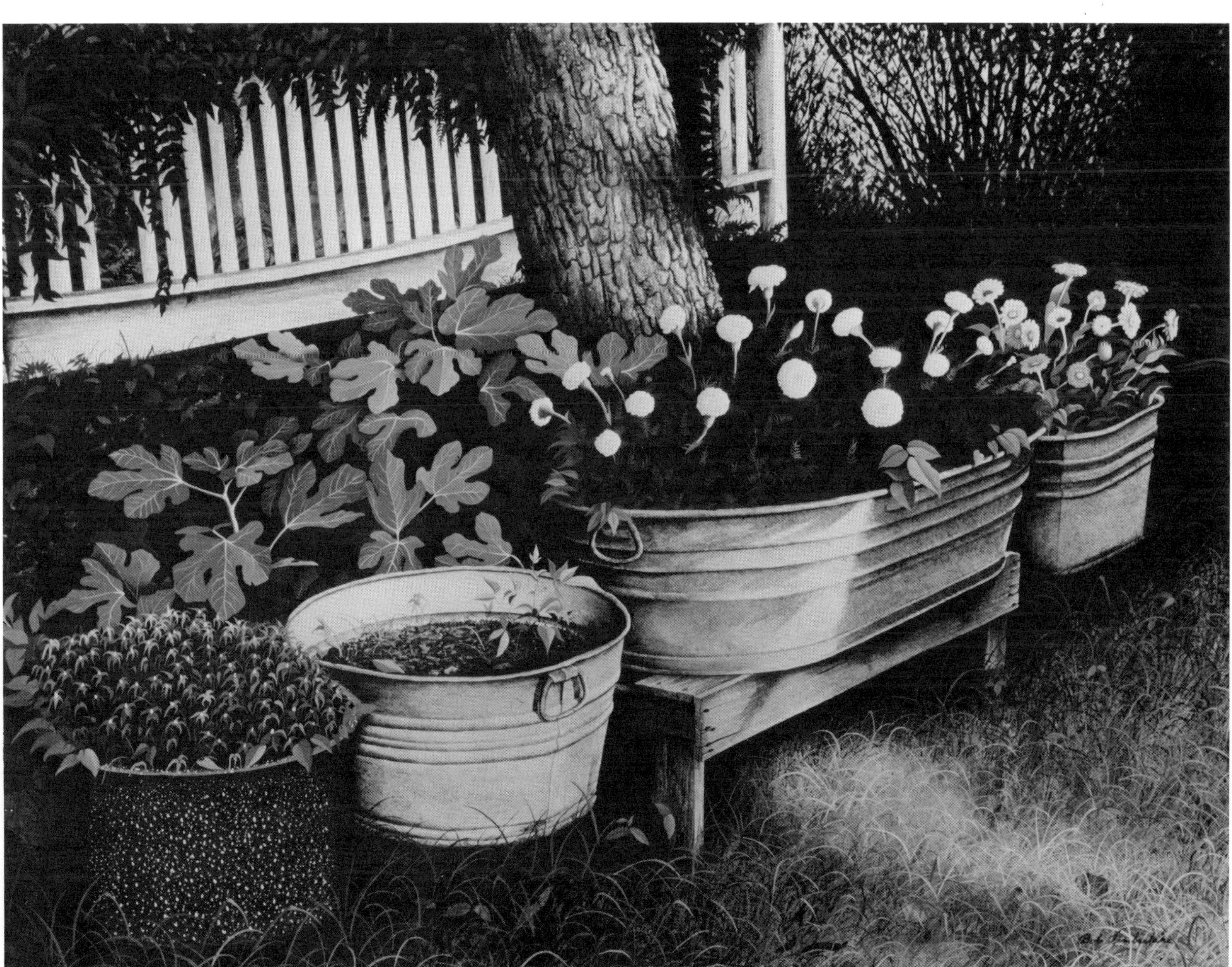

15. Wanda   1973
    Tempera   24 x 15½
    Inscribed lower left: Bob Timberlake
    Lent by Mr. and Mrs. Bob Timberlake

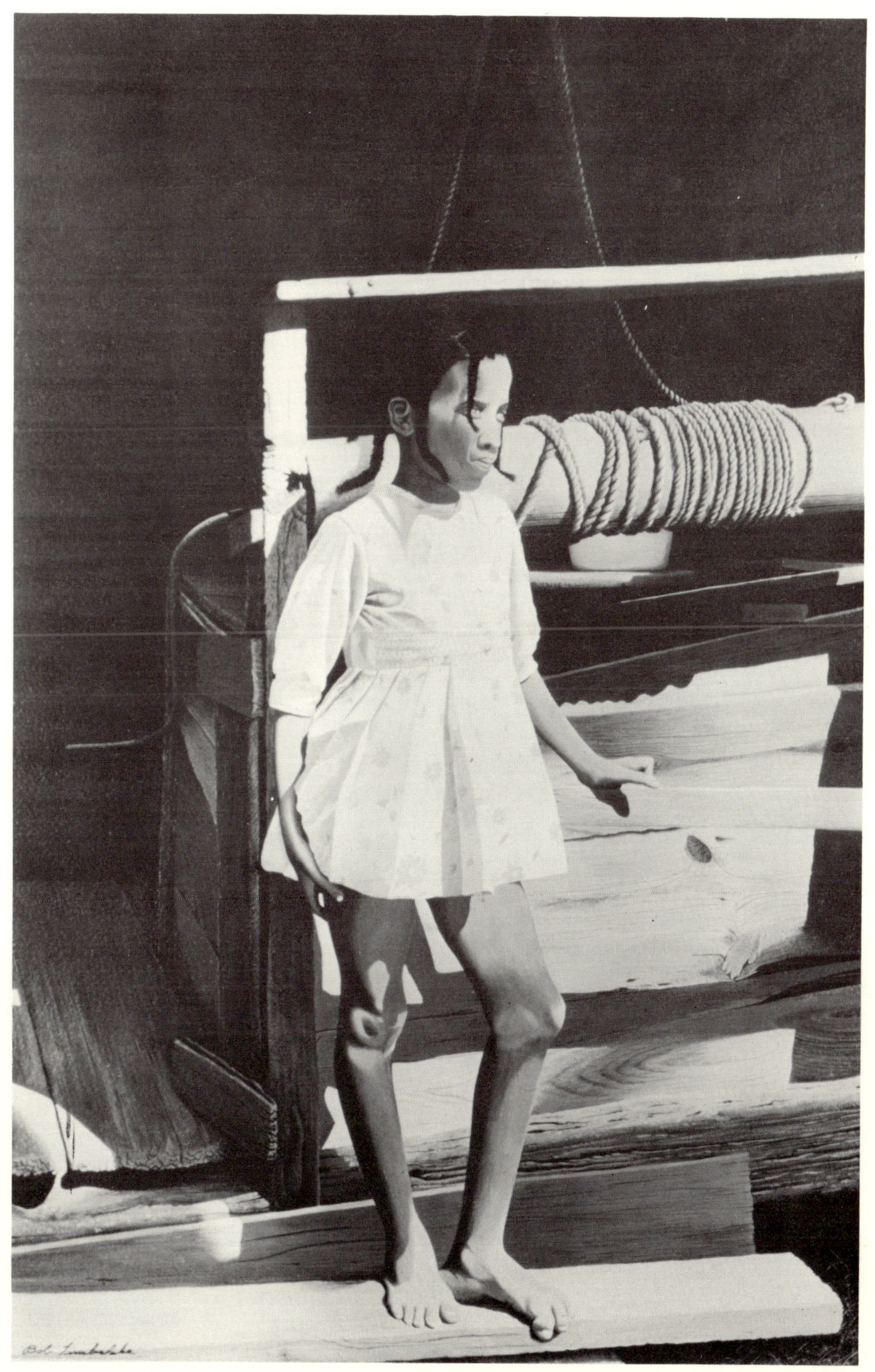

16. Kelly, Ed, and Dan   1973
    Watercolor   12½ x 20
    Inscribed upper left: Bob Timberlake
    Lent by Mr. and Mrs. Bob Timberlake

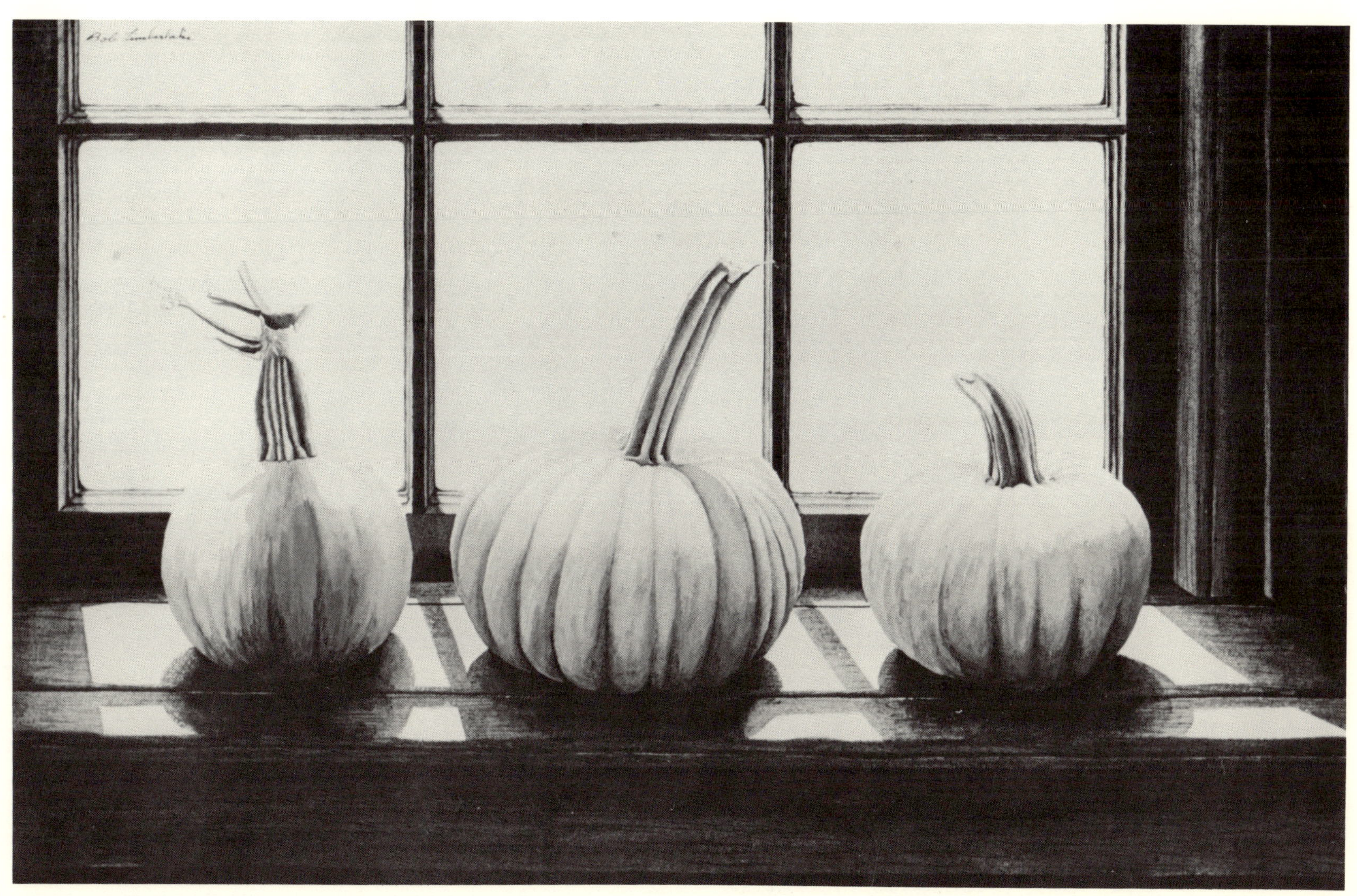

17. Mr. Zimmerman's Dairy Farm   1973
    Tempera   20½ x 30½
    Inscribed lower right: Bob Timberlake
    Lent by Mr. and Mrs. Robert L. Grubb

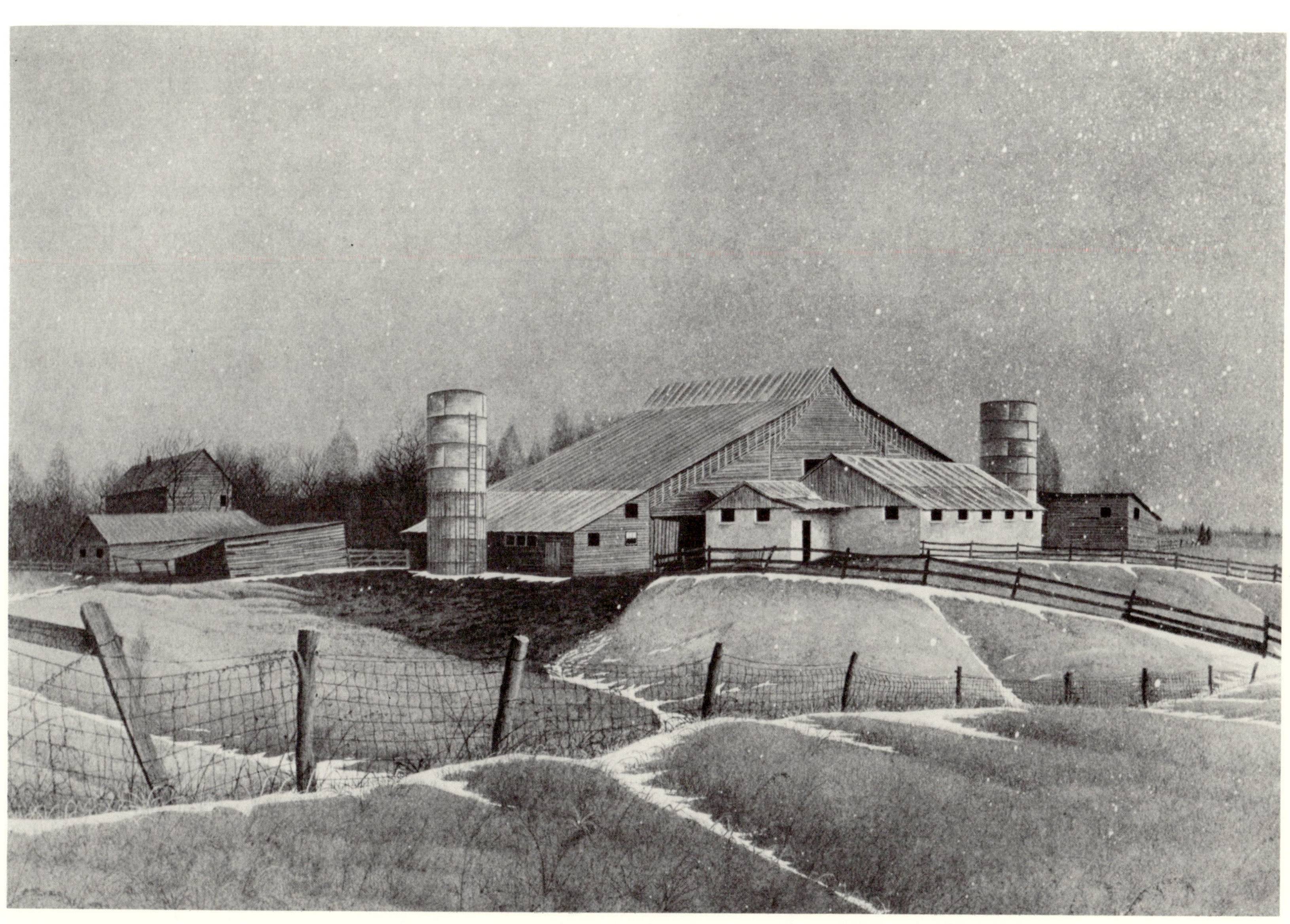

18. Spring   1974
    Watercolor   14½ x 20¼
    Inscribed lower right: Bob Timberlake
    Lent by Dr. and Mrs. David A. Roberts

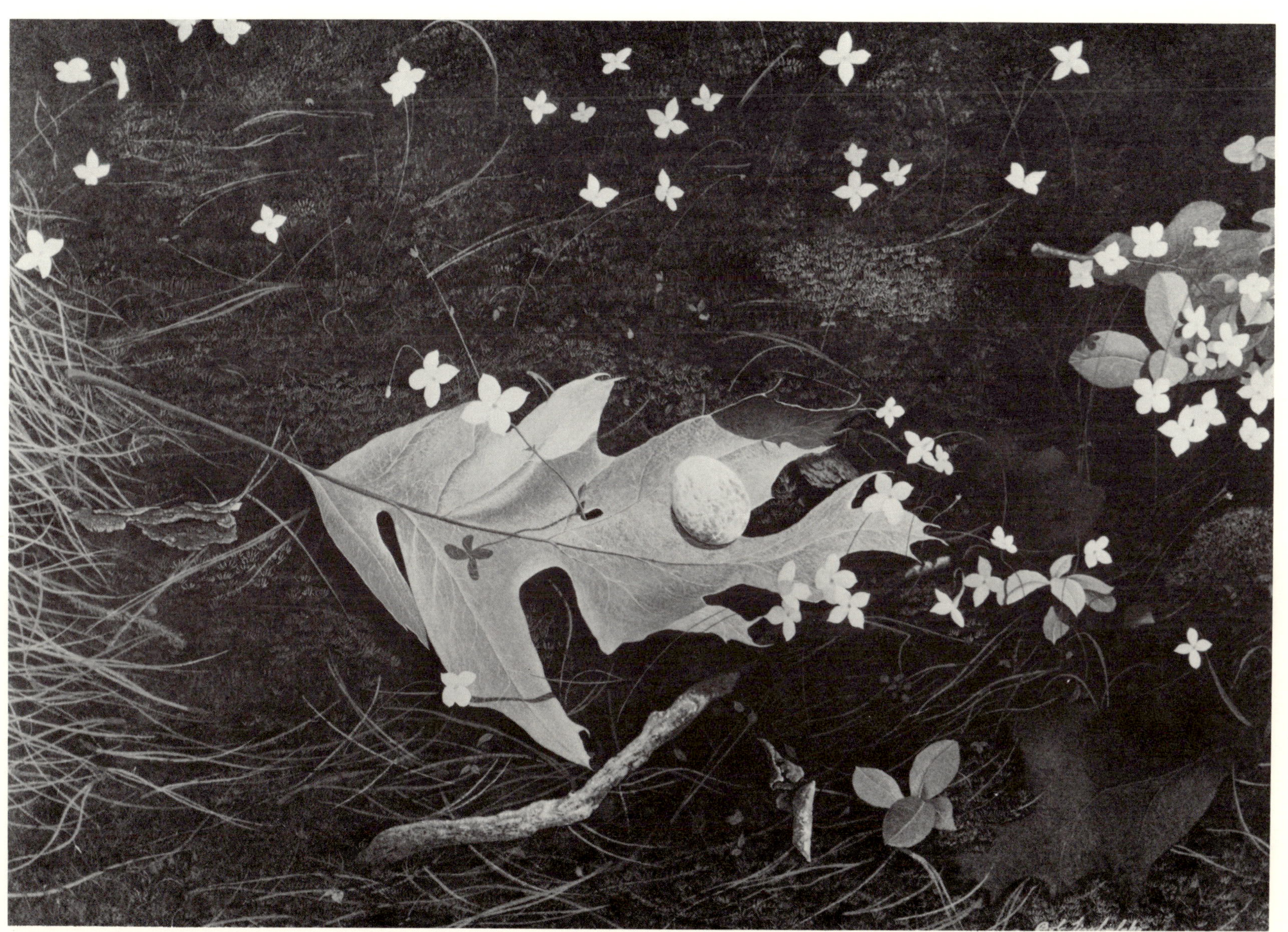

19. Woods Flowers   1974
    Watercolor   12½ x 29½
    Inscribed lower right: Bob Timberlake
    Lent by Mr. and Mrs. Frank E. Driscoll

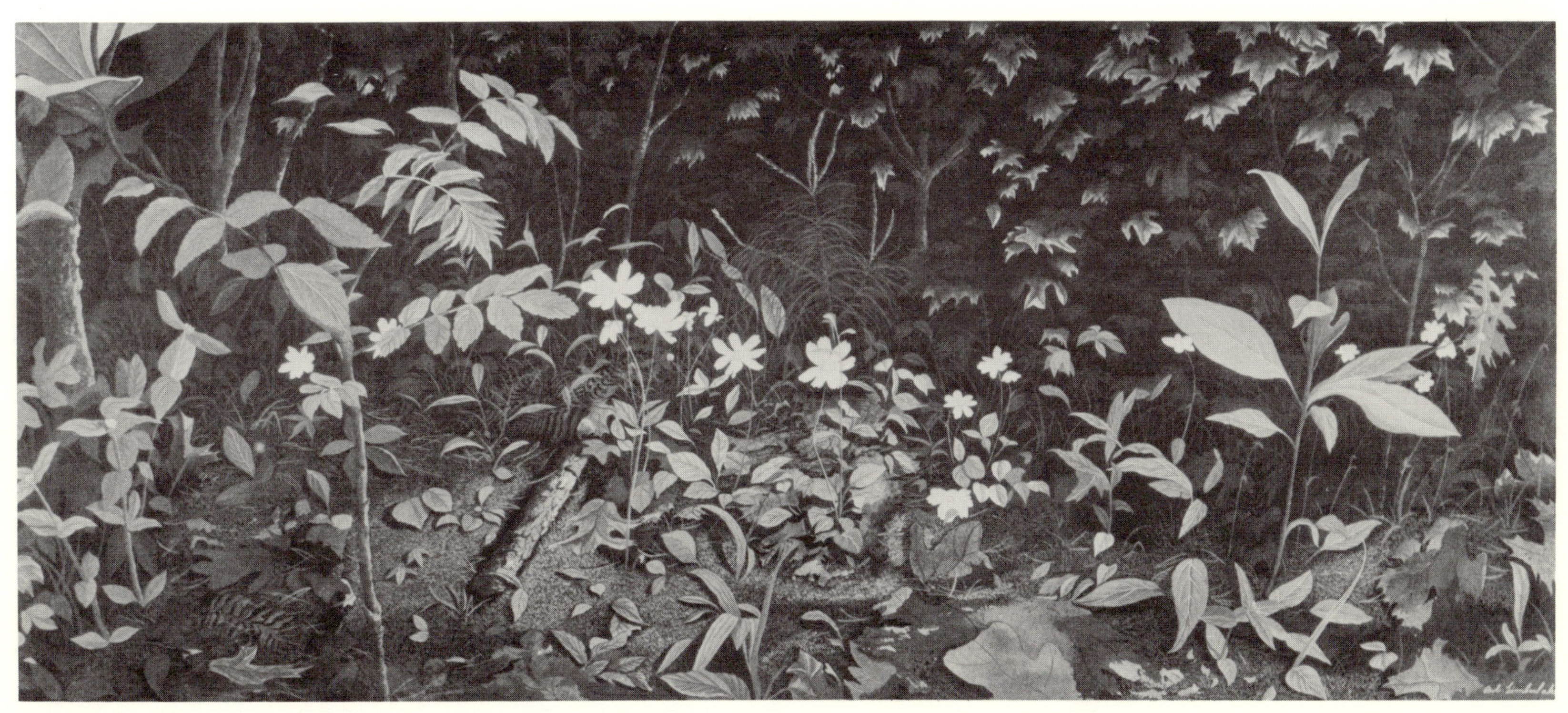

20. Wild Dog Mushroom   1974
    Watercolor   17½ x 9½
    Inscribed lower left: Bob Timberlake
    Lent by Lynn Foushee Timberlake

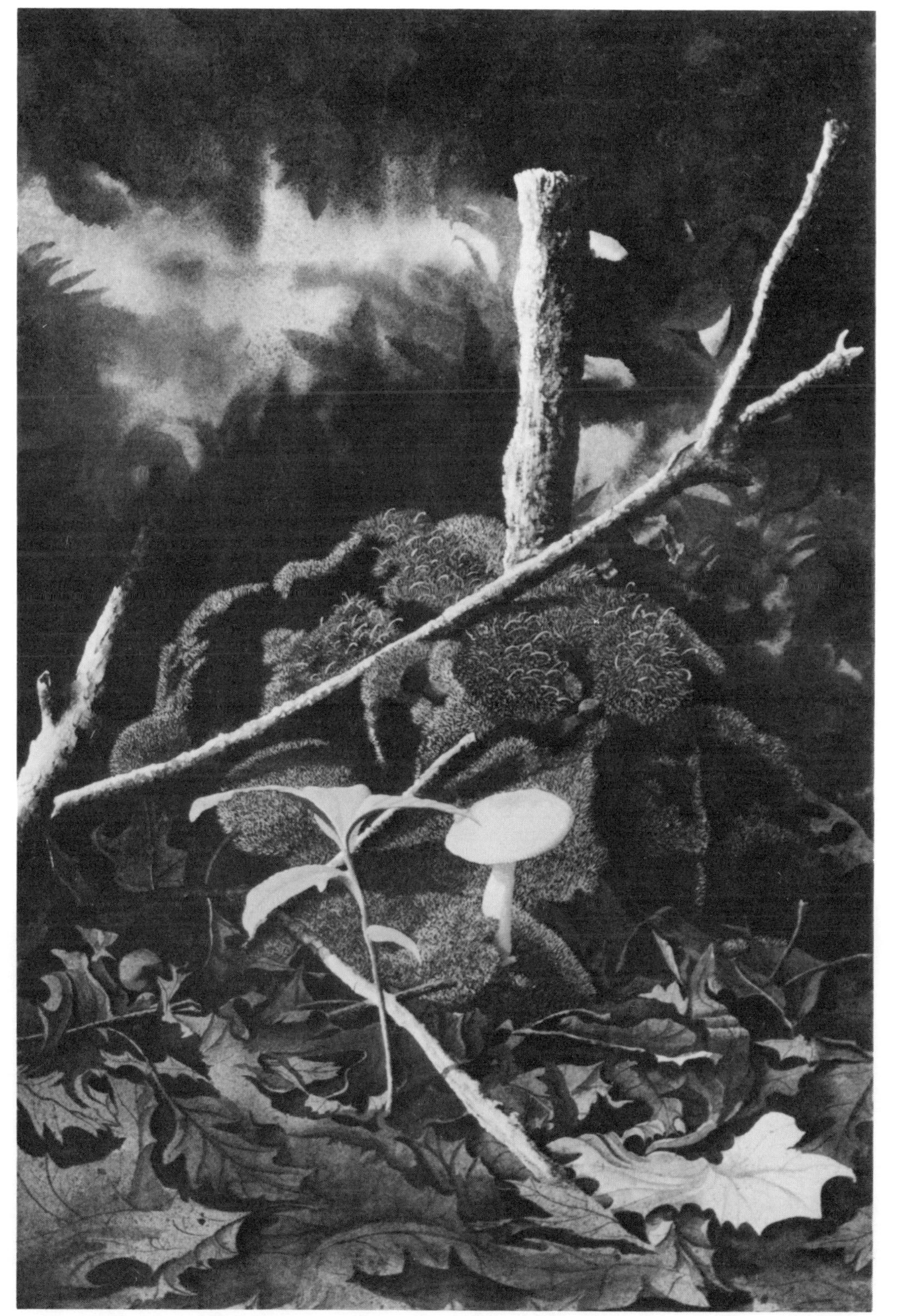

21. On The Ridge at Baldhead   1974
    Tempera   17¼ x 36½
    Inscribed lower right: Bob Timberlake
    Lent by Mr. and Mrs. Eddie Smith, Sr.

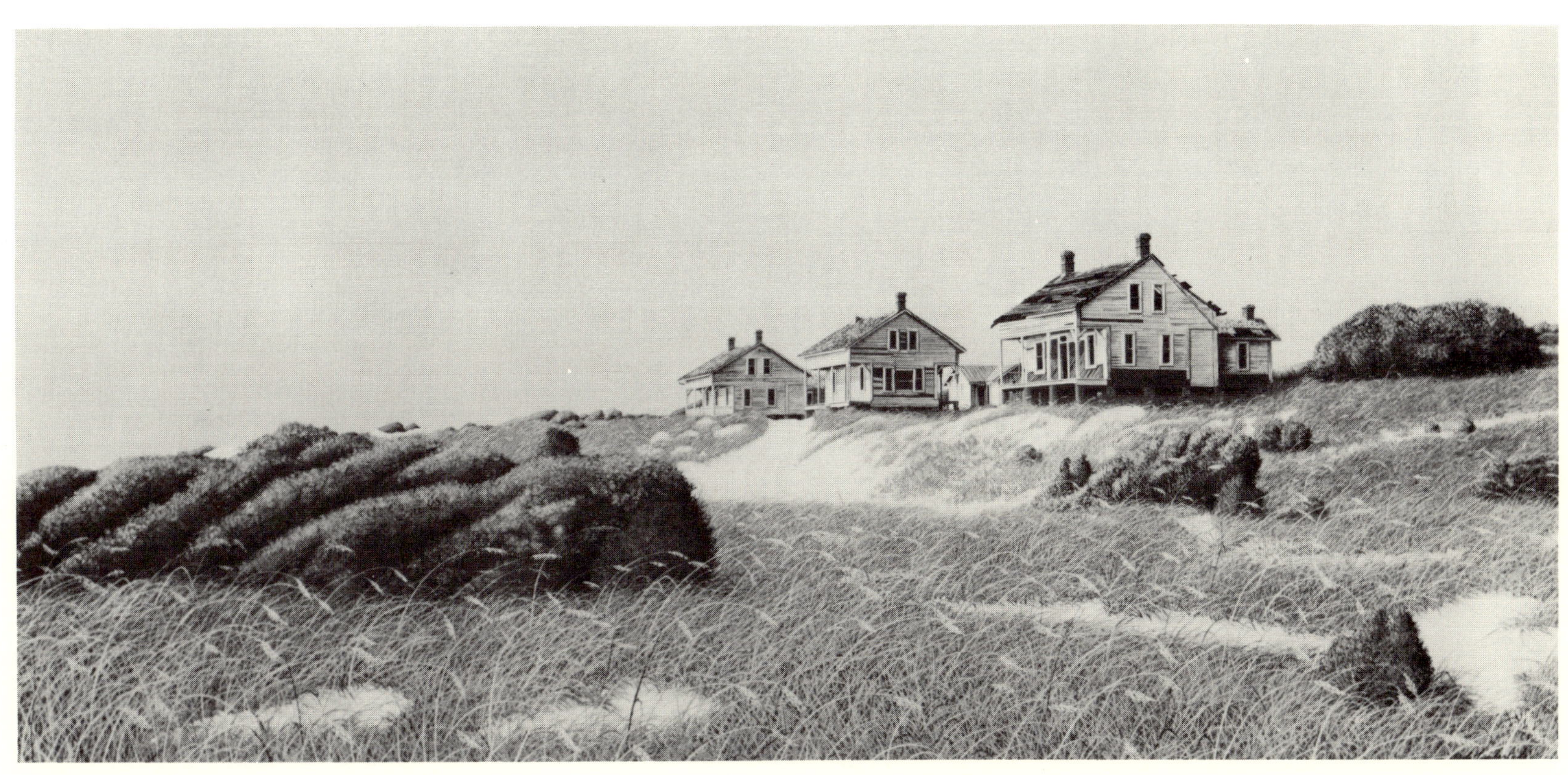

22. Front Porch   1974
    Tempera   15½ x 10
    Inscribed lower left: Bob Timberlake
    Lent by Mrs. Kay M. Timberlake

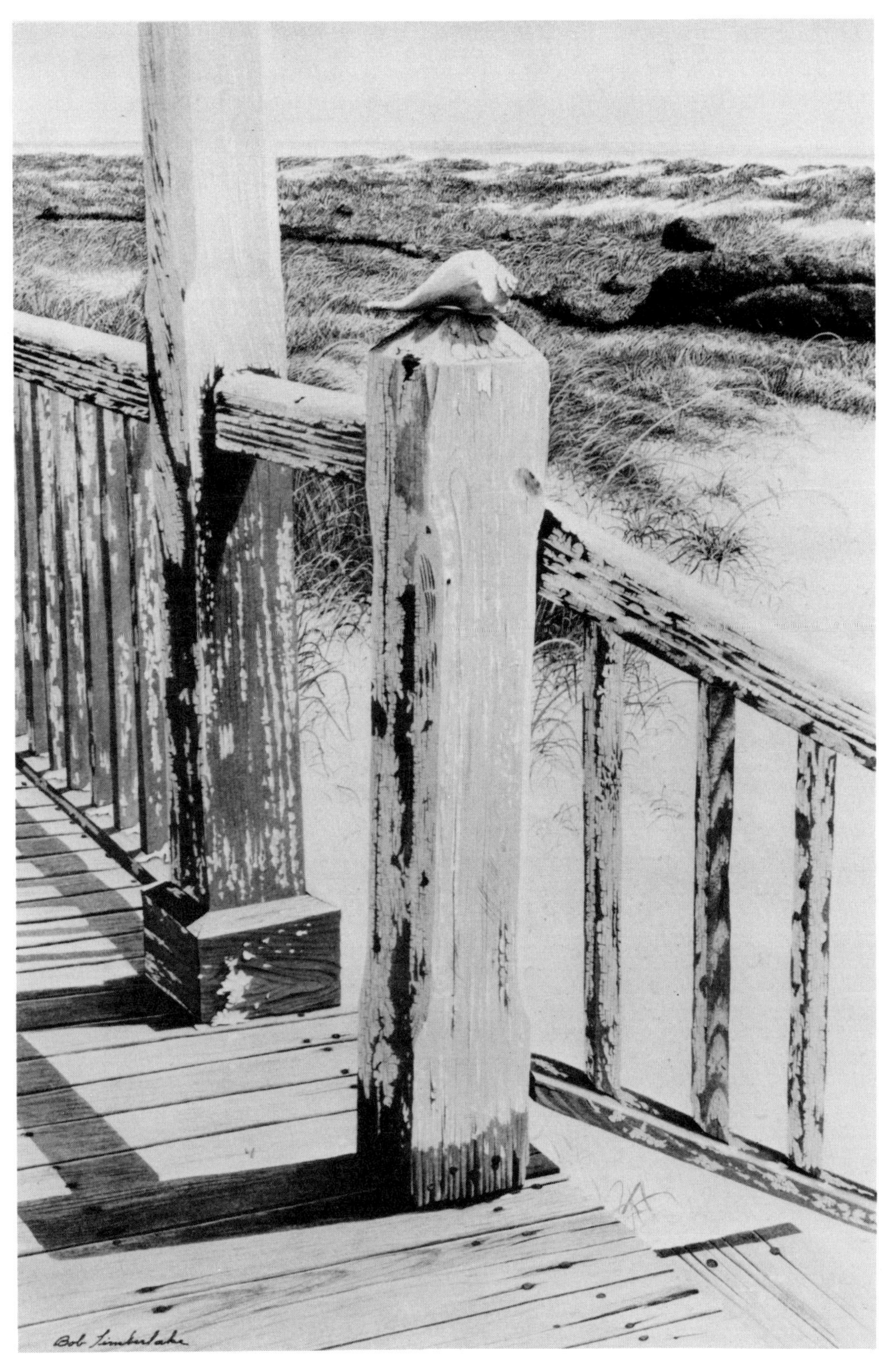

23. Study of Dan Melton   1974
    Watercolor   7 x 6
    Inscribed lower right: Bob Timberlake
    Private Collection

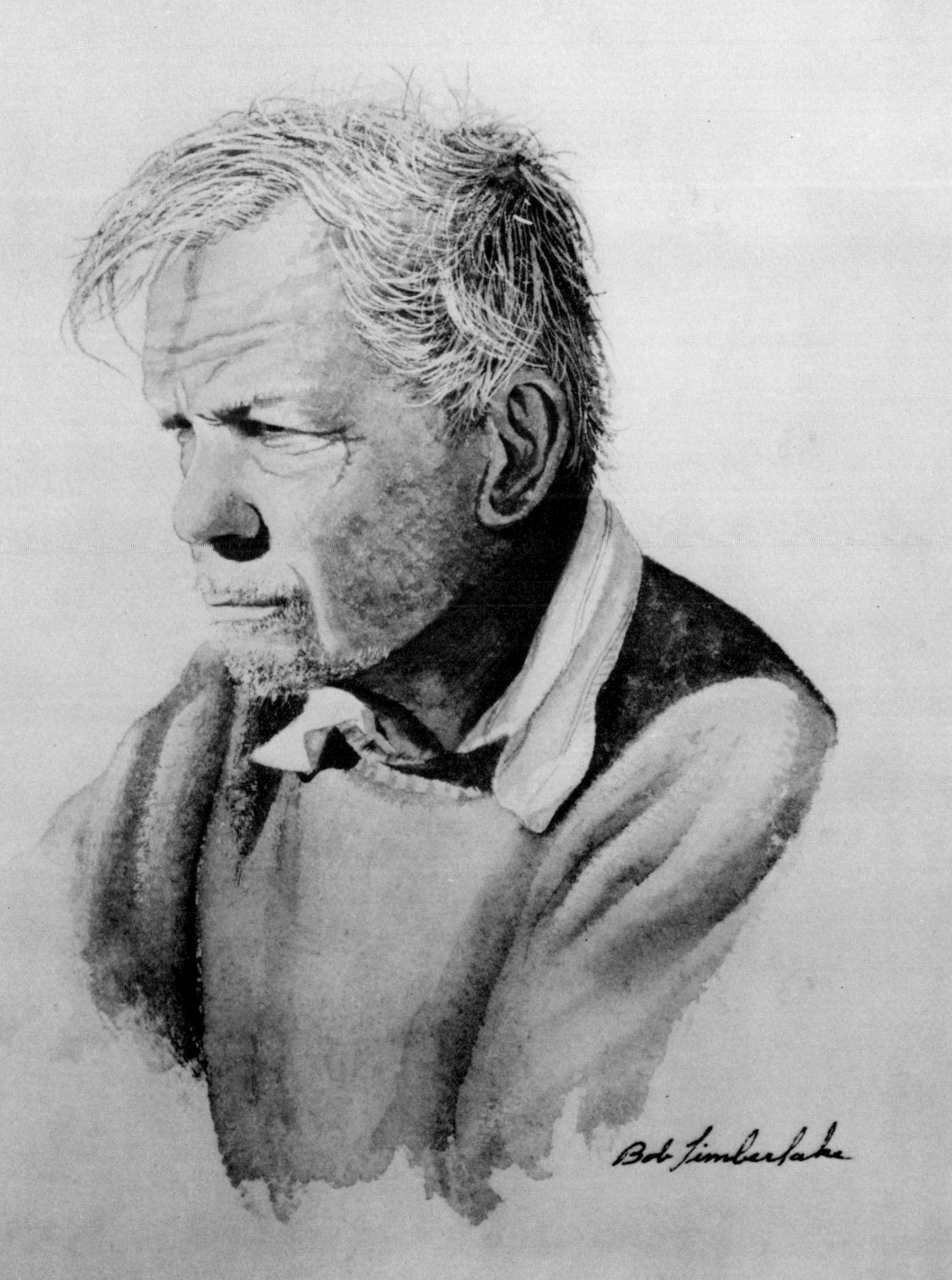

Bob Timberlake

24. Dan Melton   1974
    Tempera   16 x 12
    Inscribed lower left: Bob Timberlake
    Private Collection

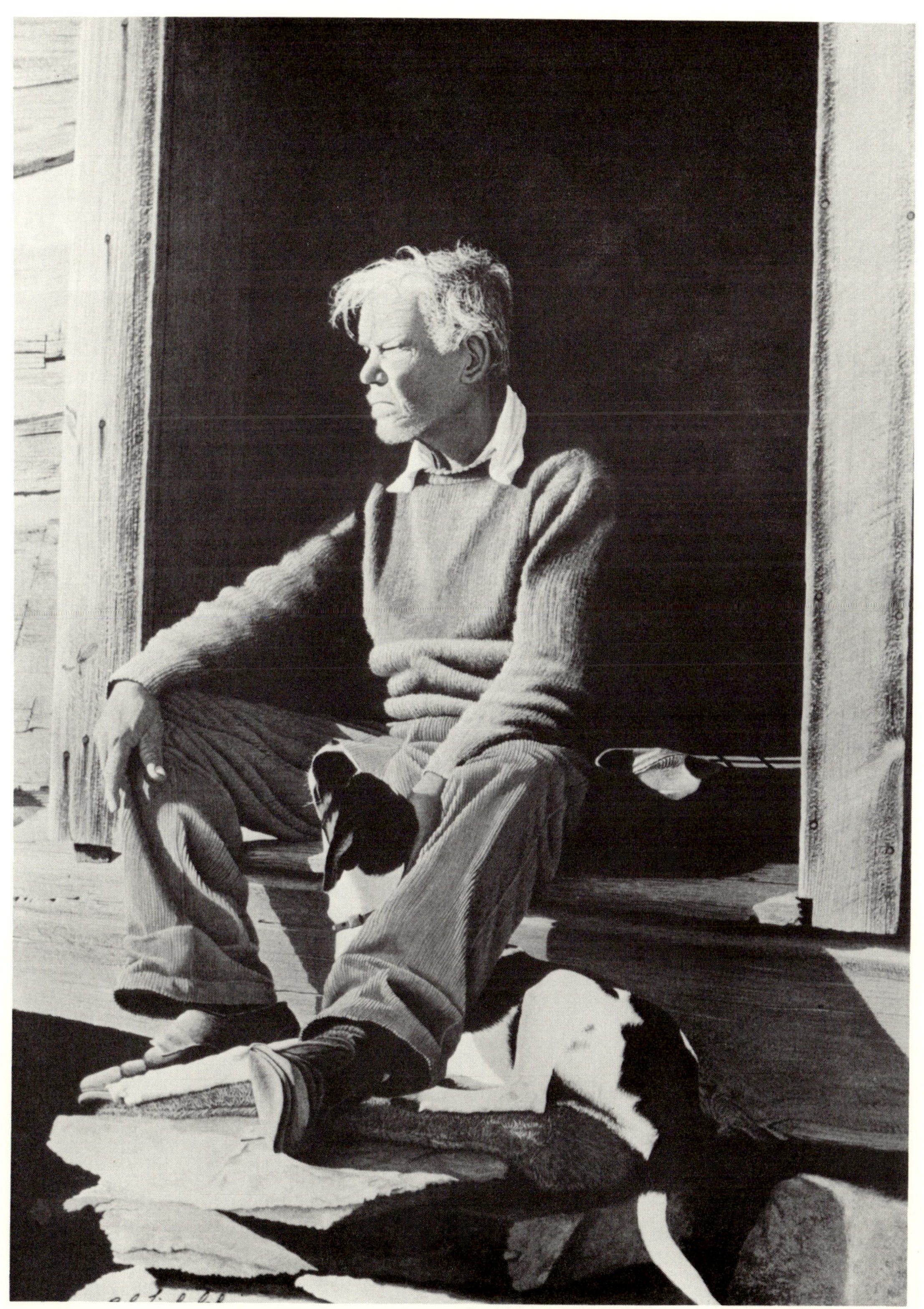

25. Mr. Petrea's Chair   1974
    Watercolor   23 x 15
    Inscribed lower right: Bob Timberlake
    Lent by Jane and Jimmy Townsend

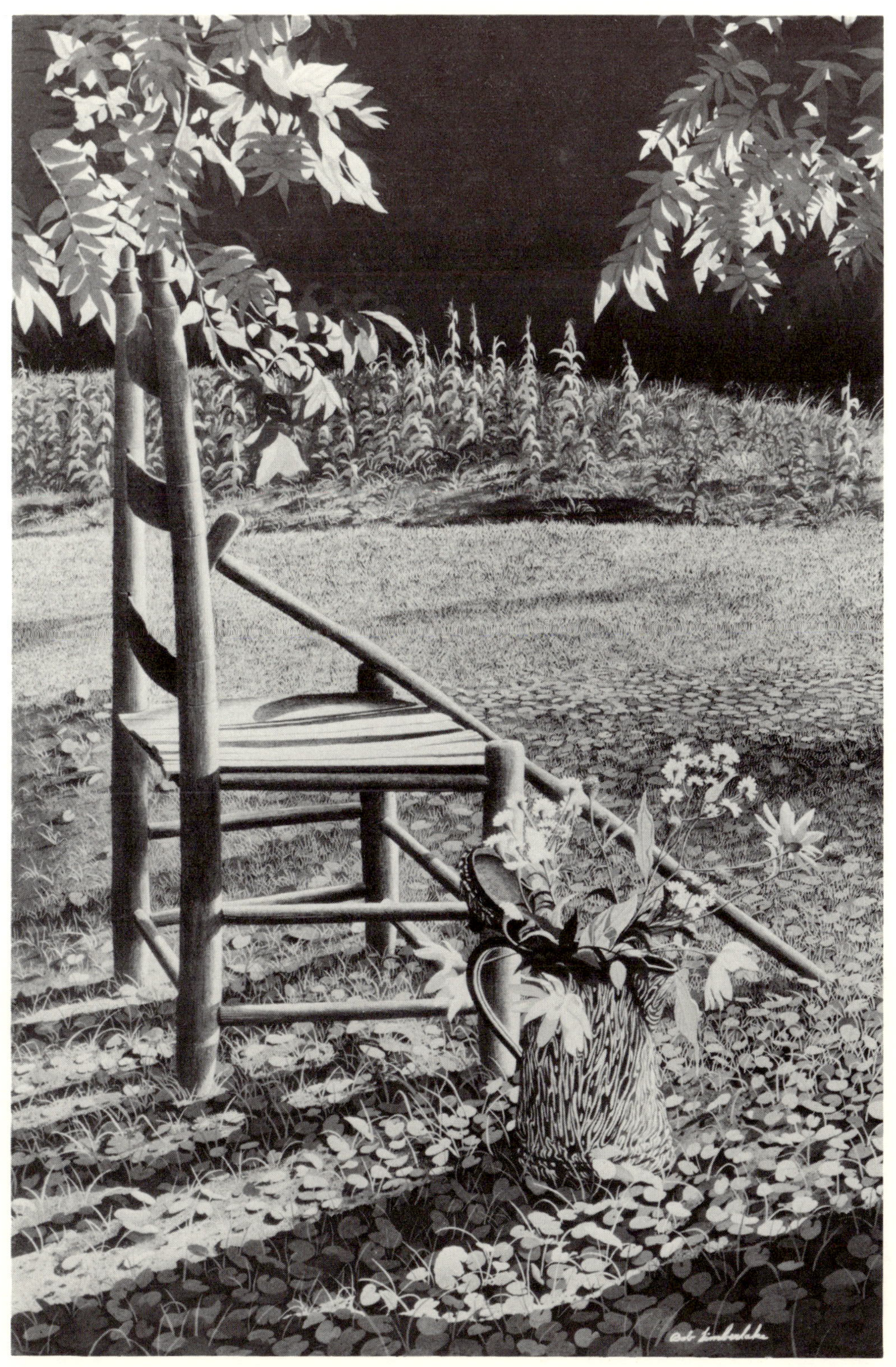

26. The Studio   1974
Tempera   18 x 40
Inscribed lower right: Bob Timberlake
Lent by The R. W. Norton Art Gallery

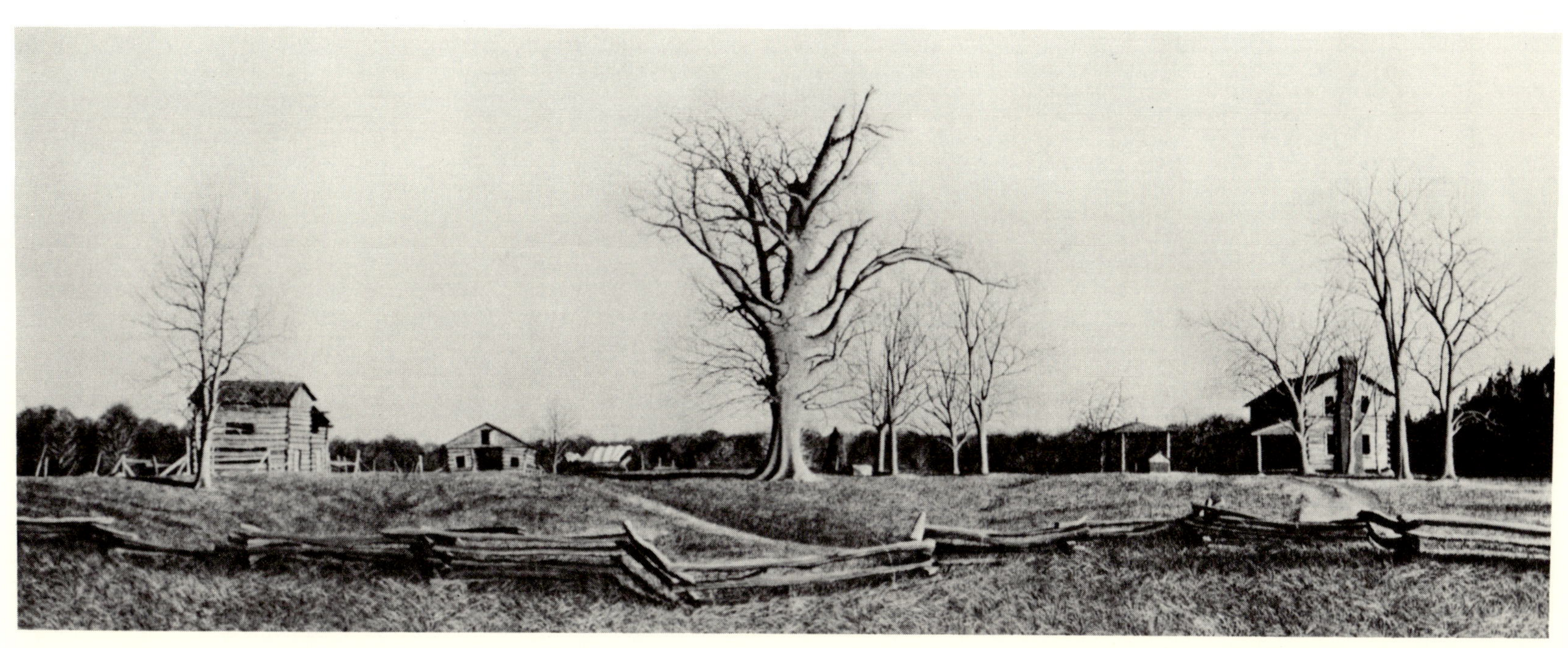

27. Pumpkins From Our Garden   1974
    Watercolor   9 x 14
    Inscribed lower left: Bob Timberlake
    Private Collection

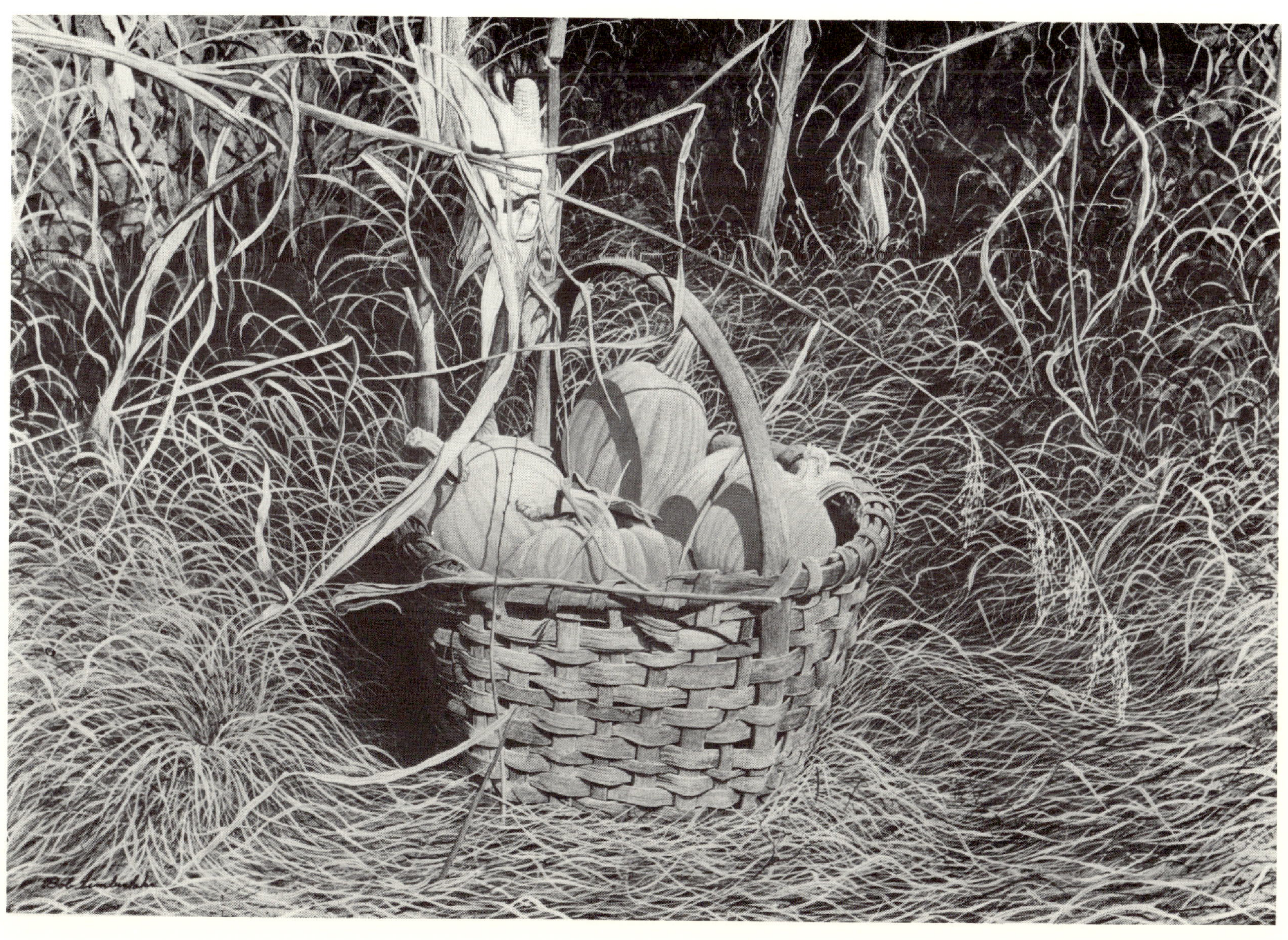

28. Another World   1974
    Watercolor   17 x 24
    Inscribed lower right: Bob Timberlake
    Private Collection

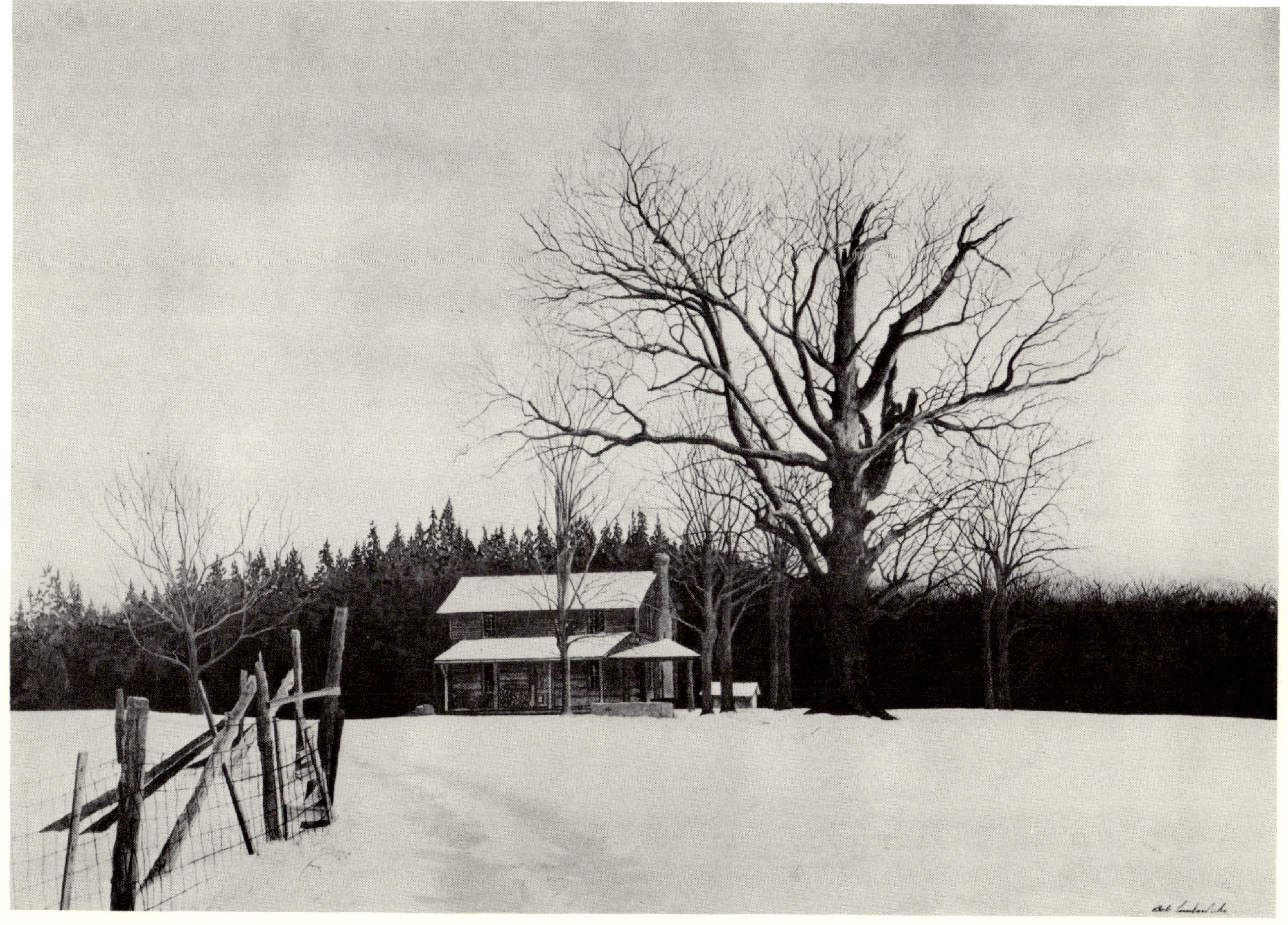

29. Rowan County   1975
    Watercolor   12 x 7
    Inscribed lower left: Bob Timberlake
    Private Collection

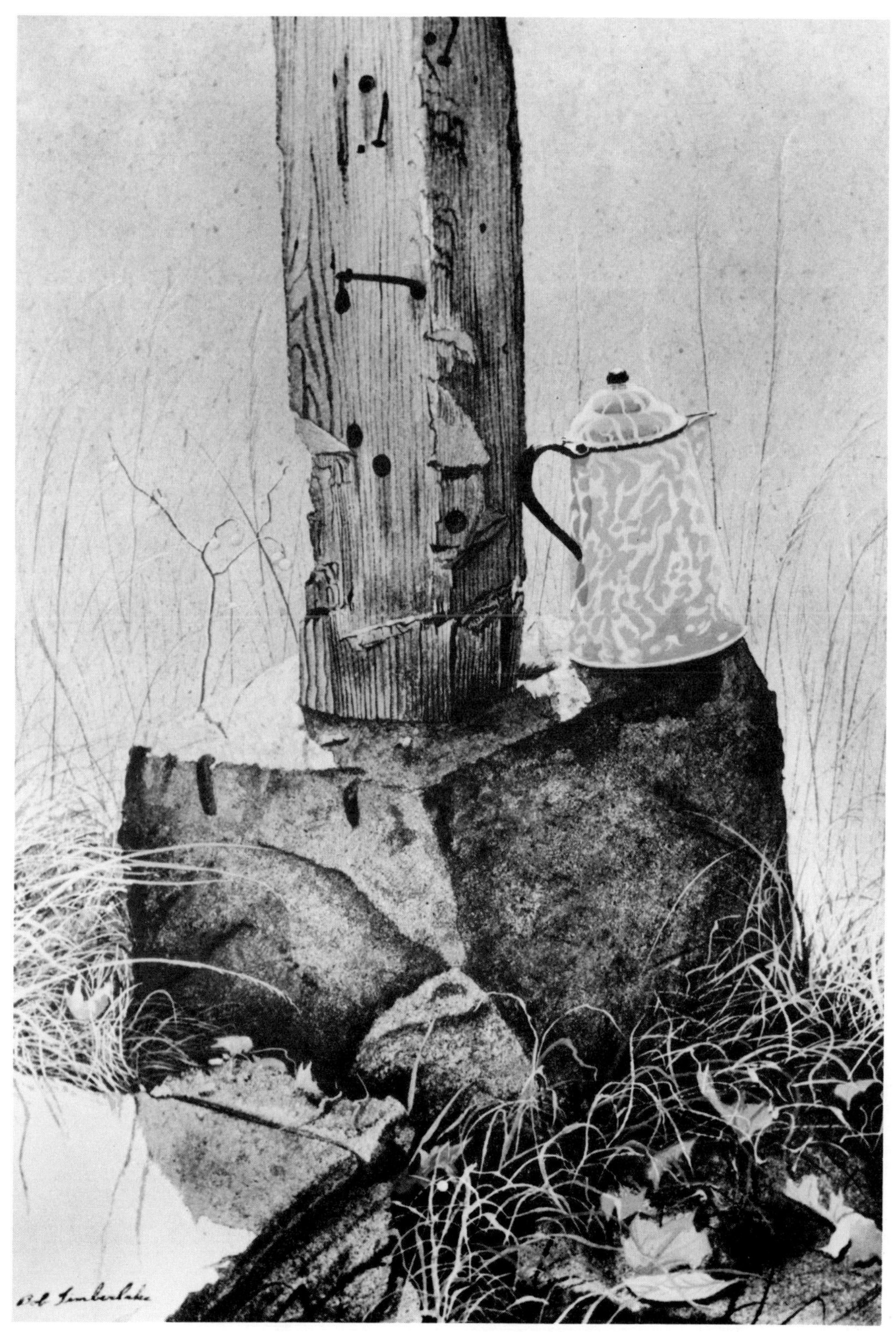

30. Watered   1975
    Watercolor   22¼ x 15
    Inscribed lower left: Bob Timberlake
    Lent by Dr. and Mrs. Joseph M. Jacobson

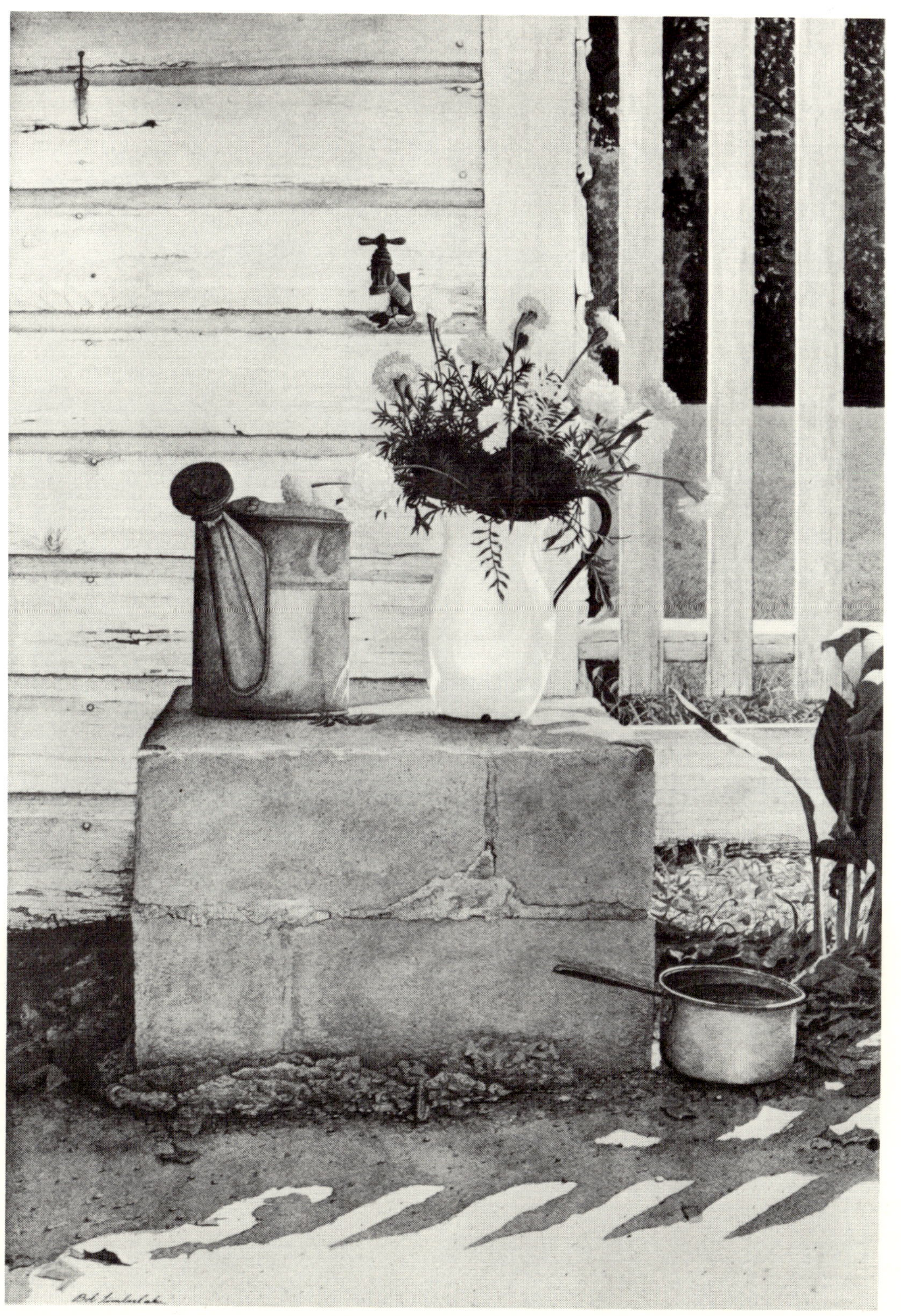

31. July   1975
    Watercolor   12⅜ x 8⅜
    Inscribed lower left: Bob Timberlake
    Lent by Dr. and Mrs. C. Richard Epes

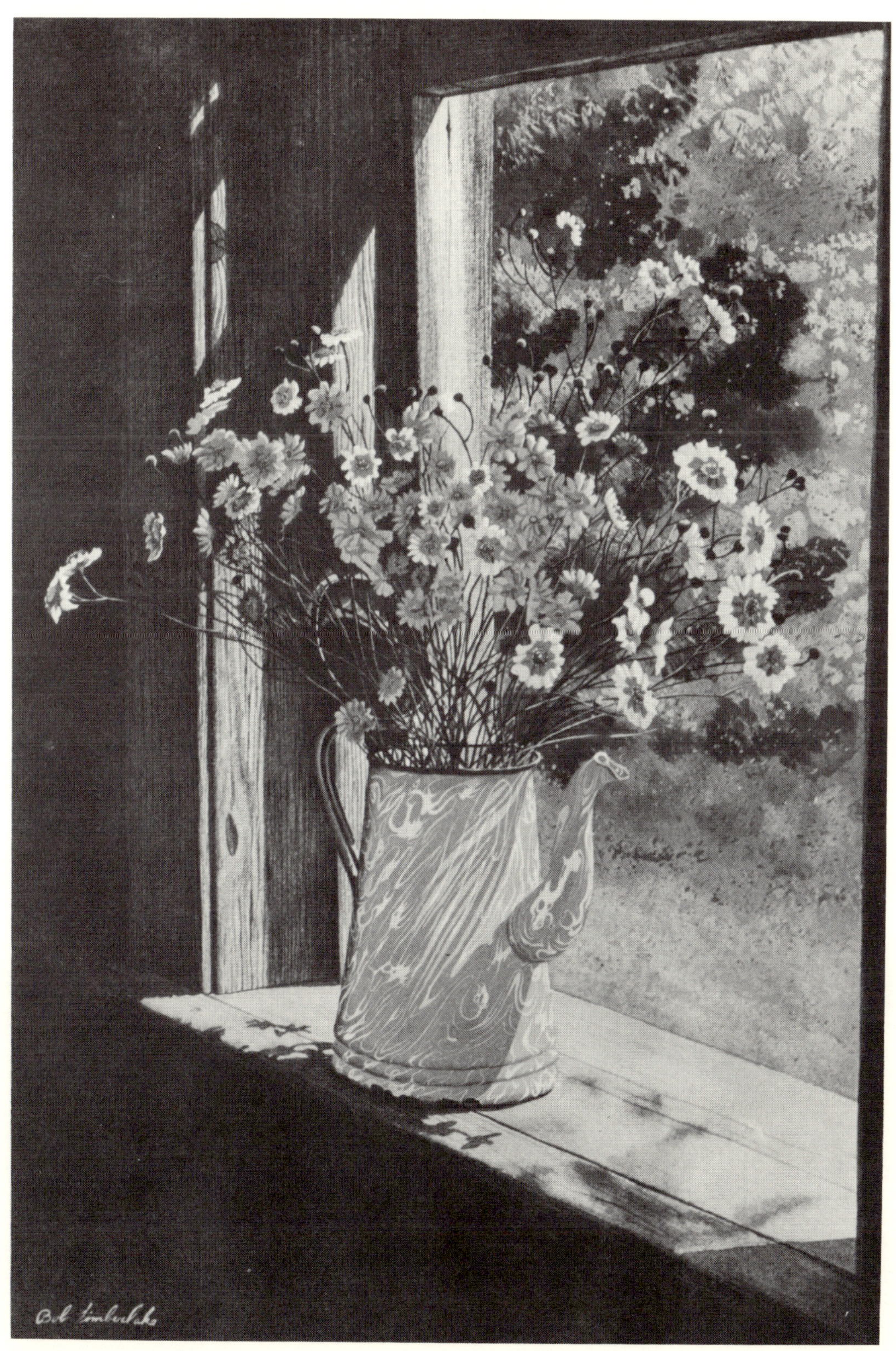

Bob Timberlake

32. Captain Charlie's View   1975
    Tempera   20¼ x 14¼
    Inscribed lower right: Bob Timberlake
    Private Collection

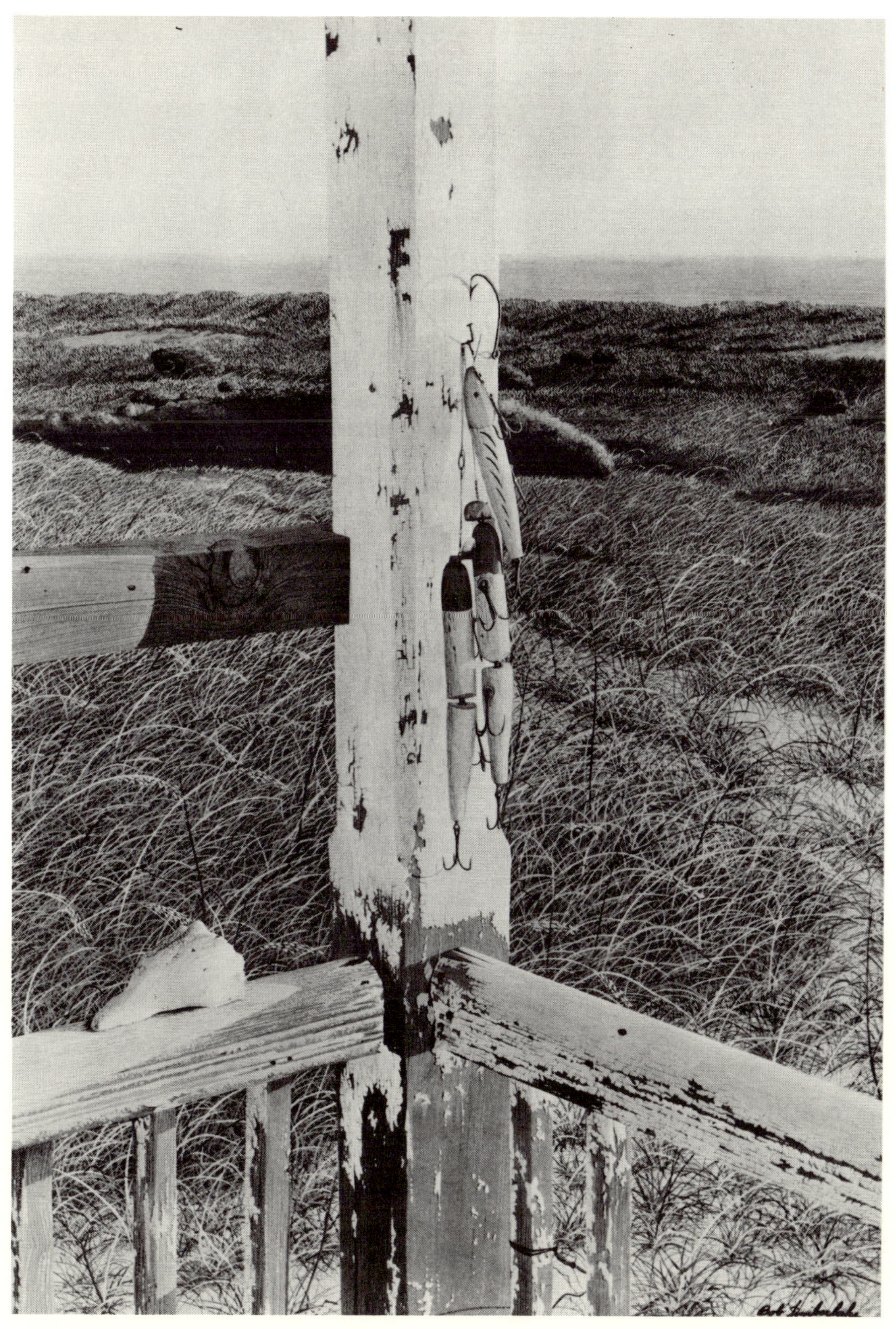

33. Geese at The Studio   1975
    Watercolor   10¼ x 18¼
    Inscribed lower right: Bob Timberlake
    Lent by Mr. and Mrs. David E. Maas

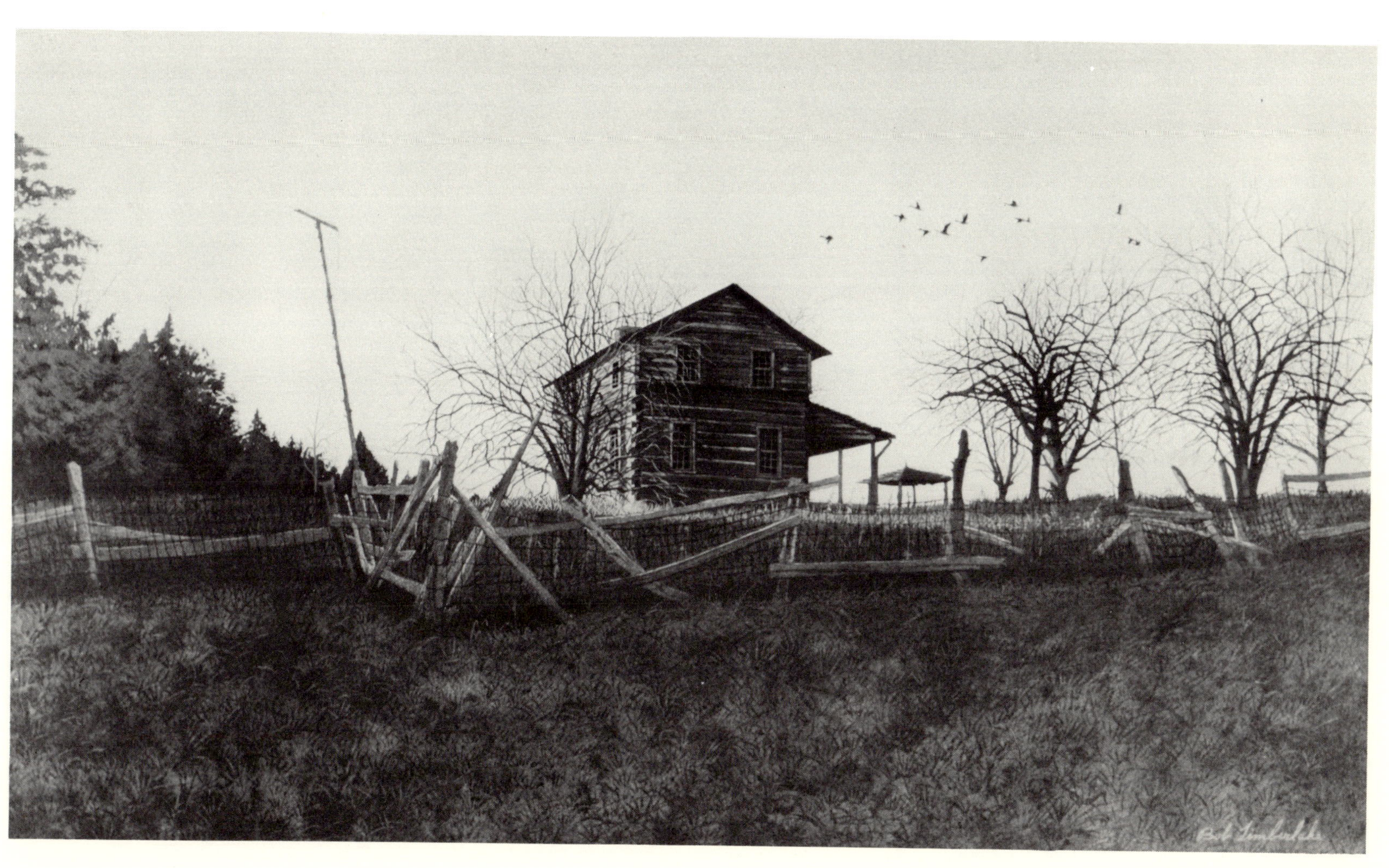

34. My Cider Barrel   1975
    Watercolor   24½ x 30
    Inscribed lower right: Bob Timberlake
    Lent by Mr. and Mrs. Daniel M. Galbreath

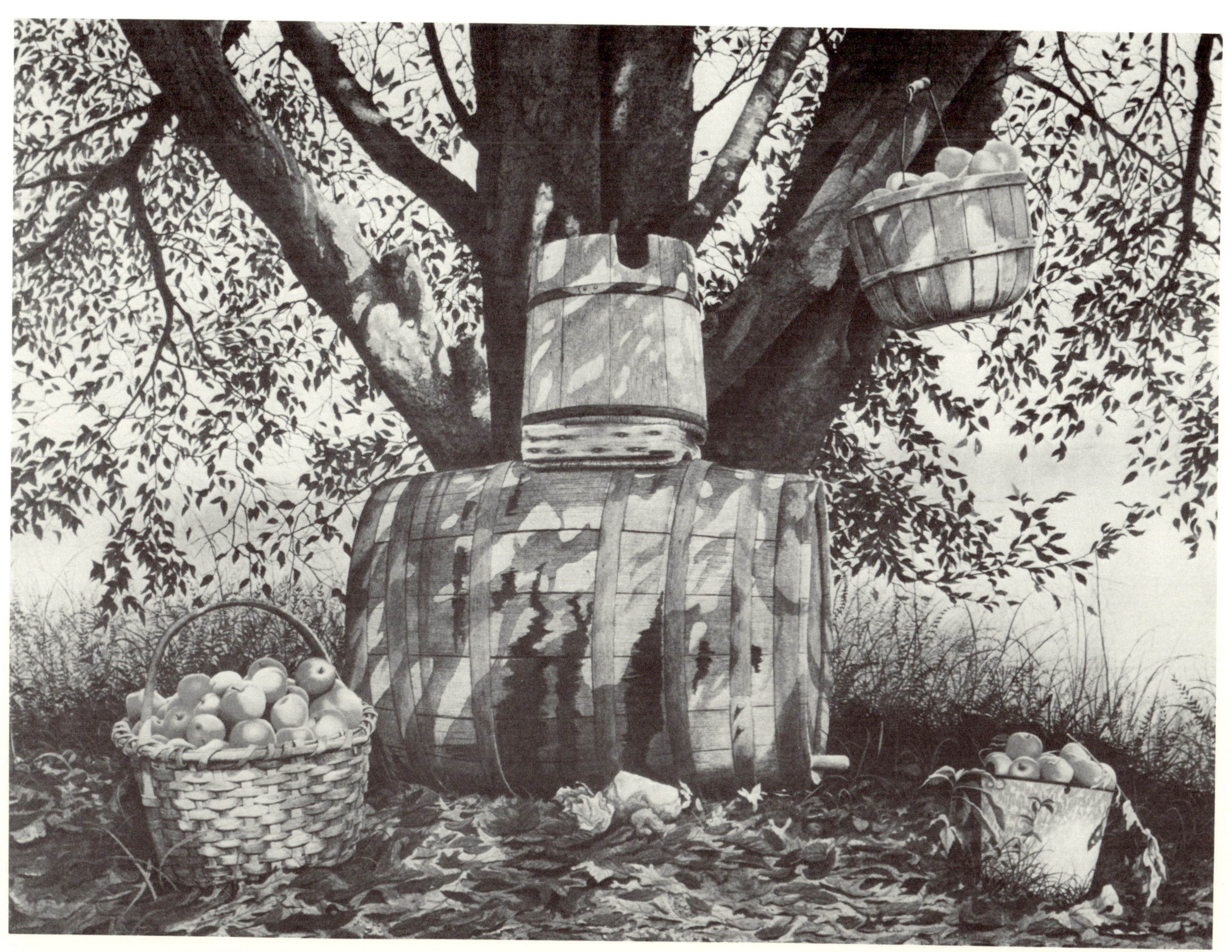

35. Gilley's House   1976
    Watercolor   30 x 22½
    Inscribed lower right: Bob Timberlake
    Lent by Federal Reserve Bank of Richmond

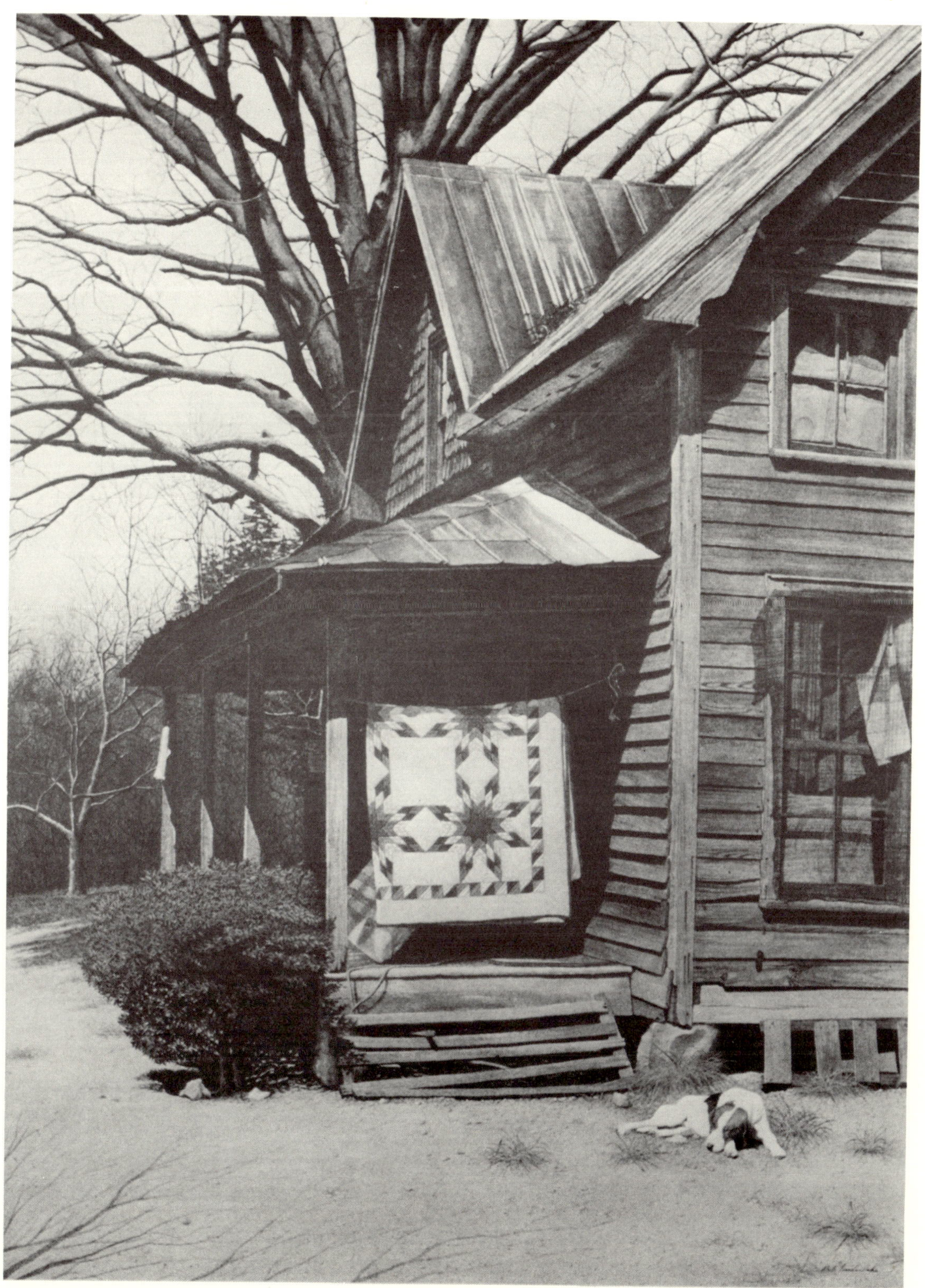

36. October Persimmons   1976
    Watercolor   14 x 11
    Inscribed lower right: Bob Timberlake
    Lent by Mrs. Marlot H. Phillips

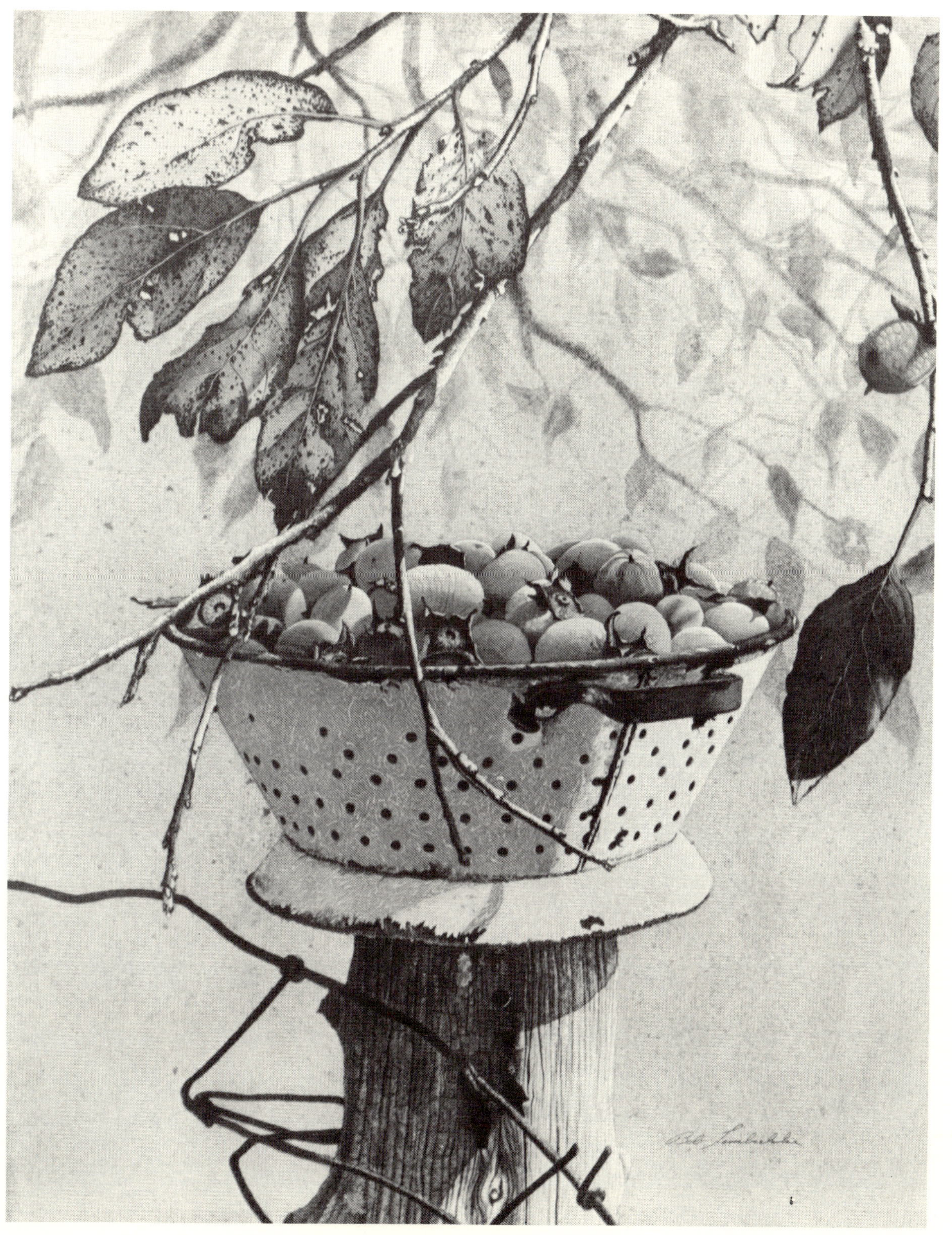

37. Mr. Zimmerman's Corn   1979
    Watercolor   15 x 22¼
    Inscribed lower right: Bob Timberlake
    Lent by Dr. and Mrs. C. Richard Epes

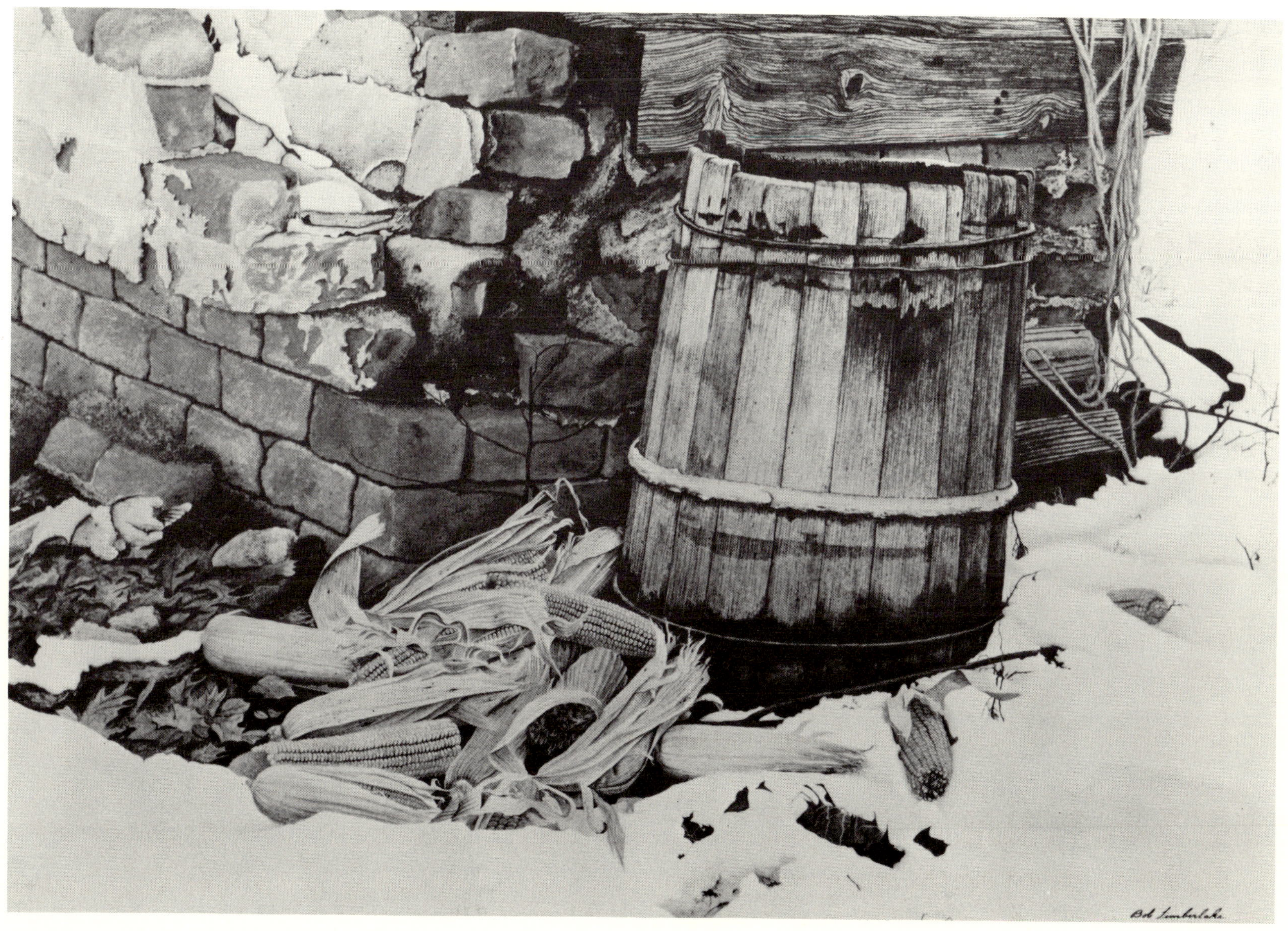

Bob Timberlake

38. Snow World   1976
    Watercolor   22¼ x 15
    Inscribed lower right: Bob Timberlake
    Lent by Mr. and Mrs. Douglas E. Ix

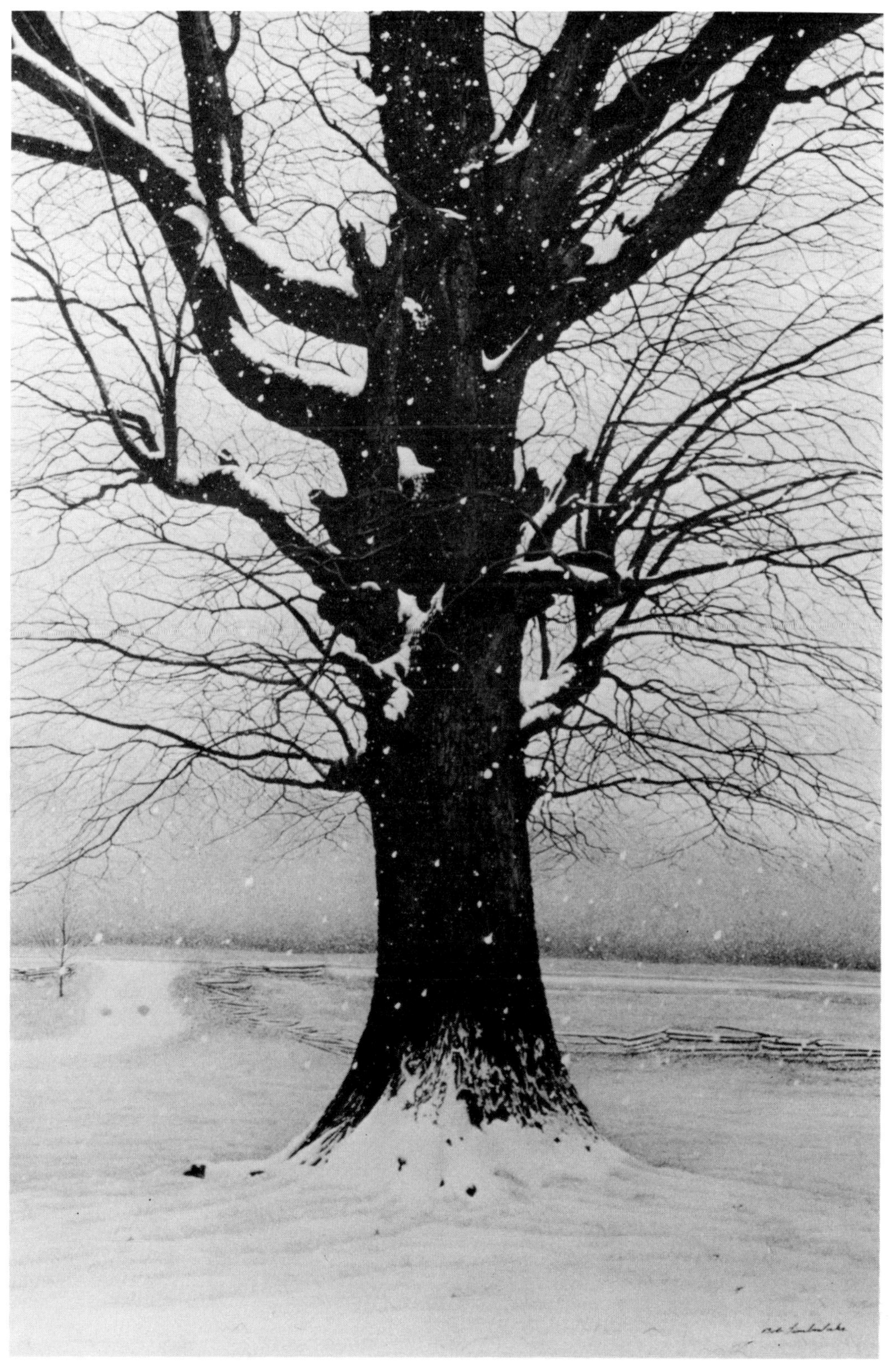

39. Knott's Island Decoys　　1977
　　Watercolor　15½ x 22¼
　　Inscribed lower right: Bob Timberlake
　　Private Collection

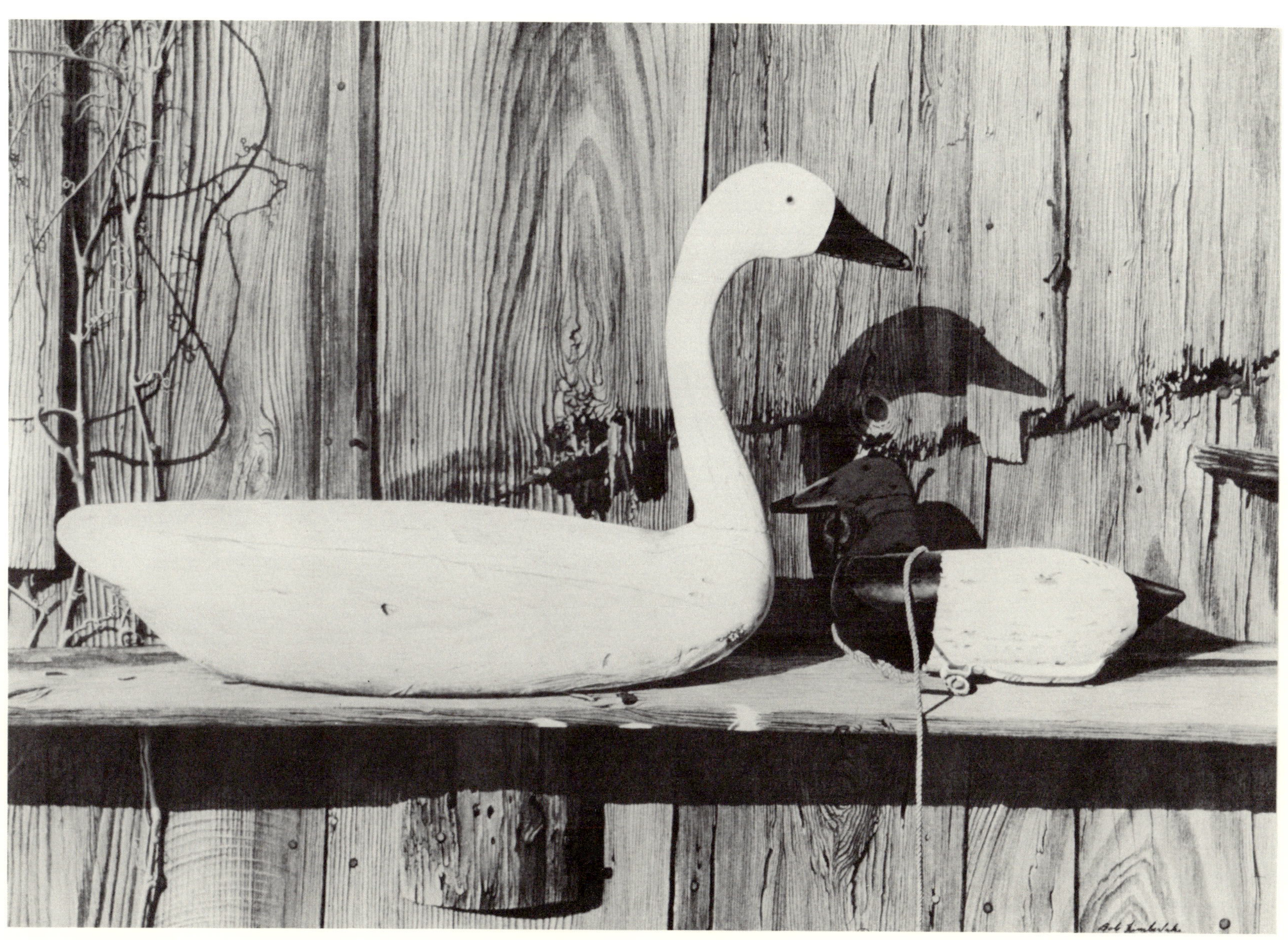

40. Studio Geraniums   1977
    Watercolor   30½ x 22½
    Inscribed lower right: Bob Timberlake
    Private Collection

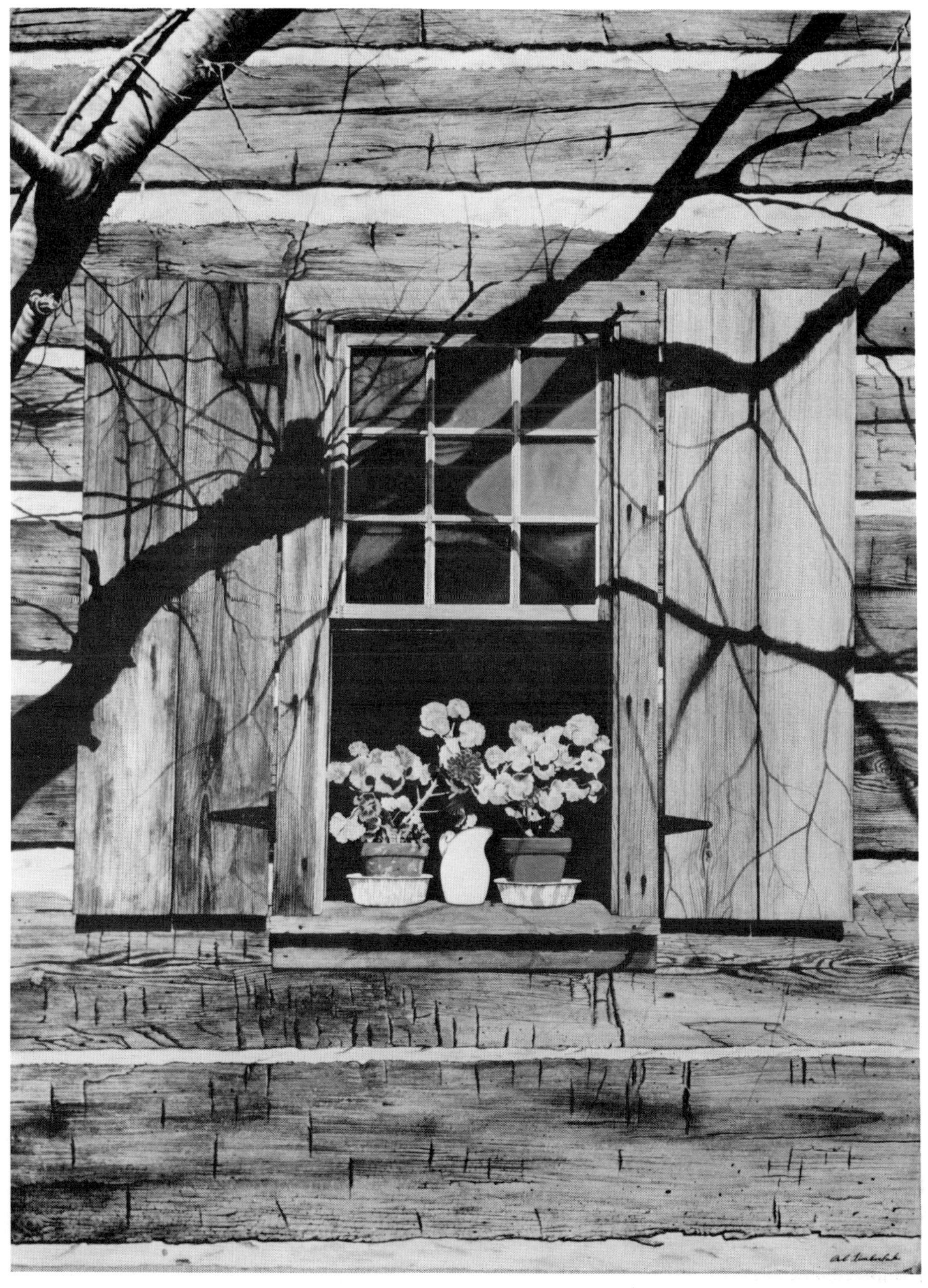

41. Aunt Buff's Quilt   1977
    Tempera   16 x 30
    Inscribed lower right: Bob Timberlake
    Lent by Jane and Jimmy Townsend

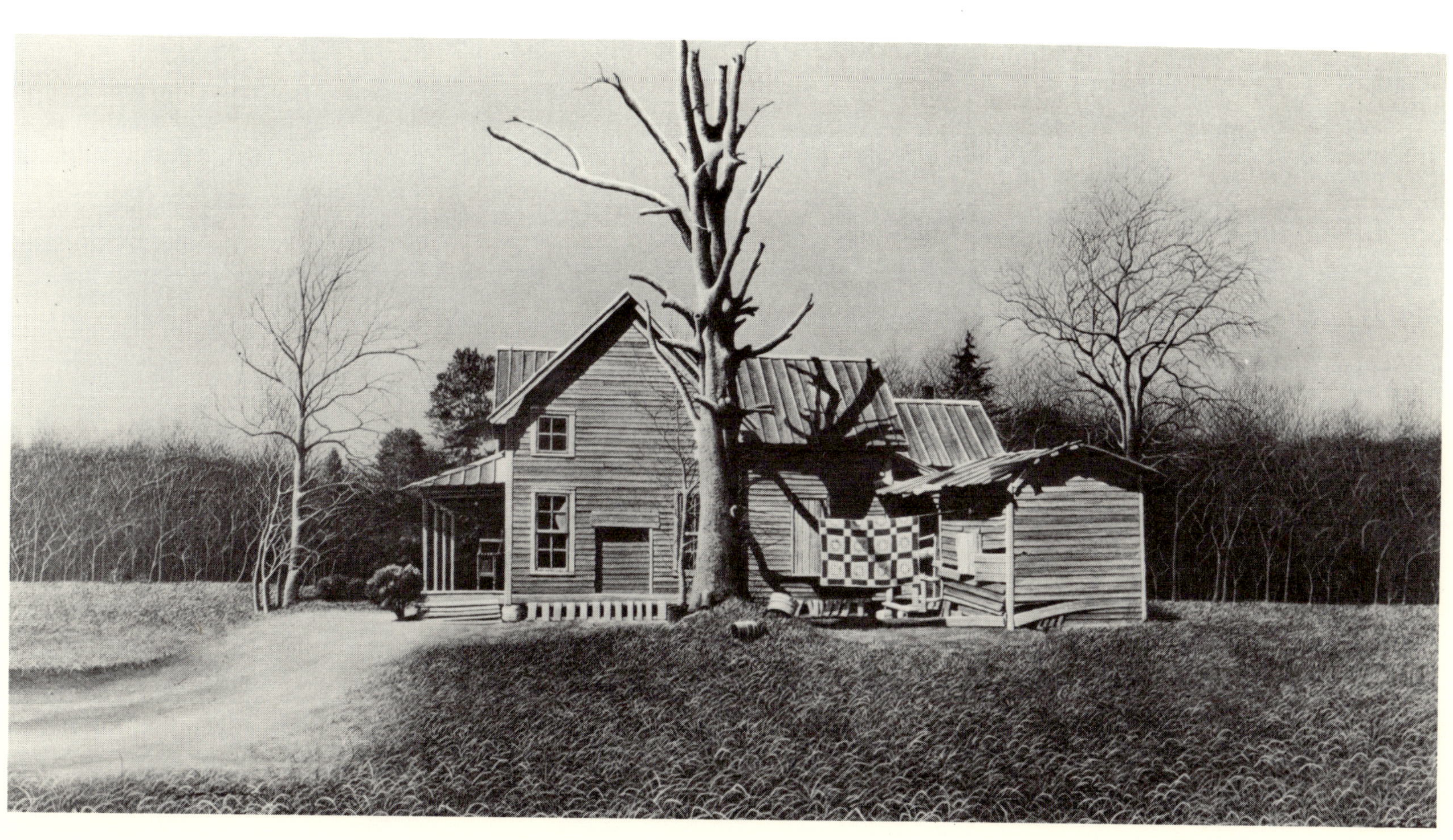

42. South Carolina's Heritage   1977
    Watercolor   30 x 22¼
    Inscribed lower right: Bob Timberlake
    Lent by Mr. and Mrs. C. H. Timberlake, Sr.

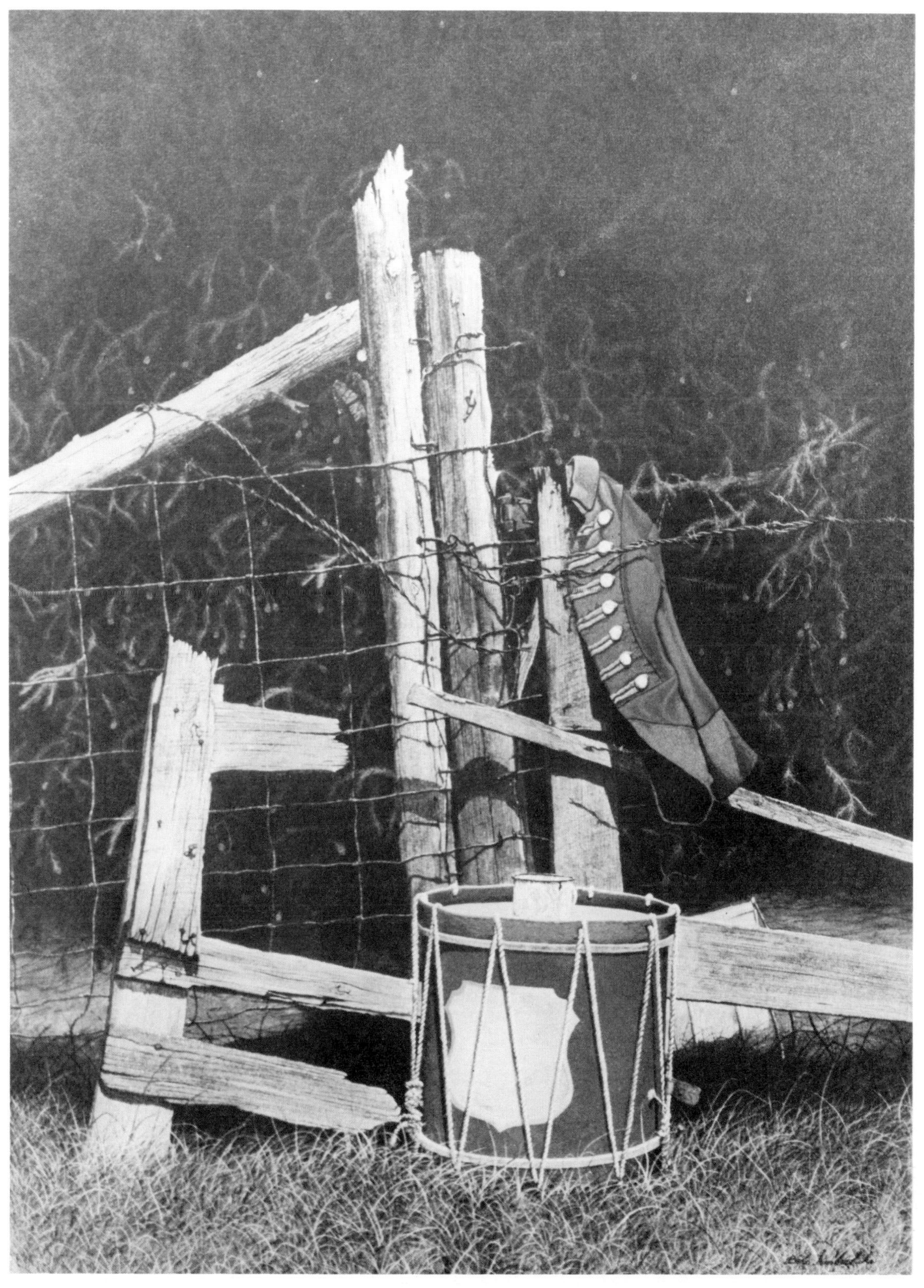

43. Daisies   1978
    Watercolor   15½ x 22¼
    Inscribed lower right: Bob Timberlake
    Lent by Mr. and Mrs. Robert L. Smith

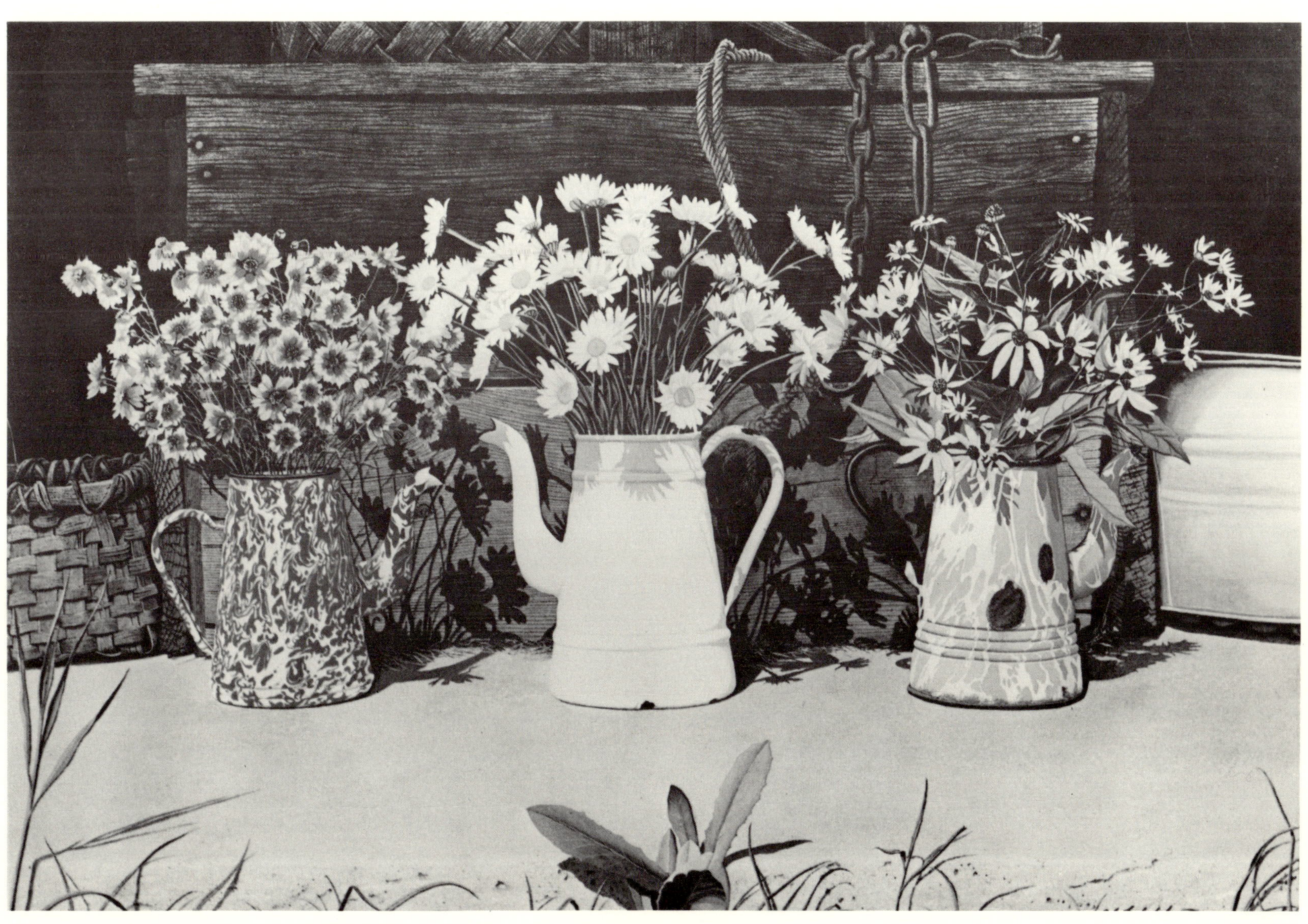

44. Study for Grubb's Gazebo   1978
    Pencil   11 x 8
    Inscribed lower right: Bob Timberlake
    Lent by Mr. and Mrs. Robert L. Grubb

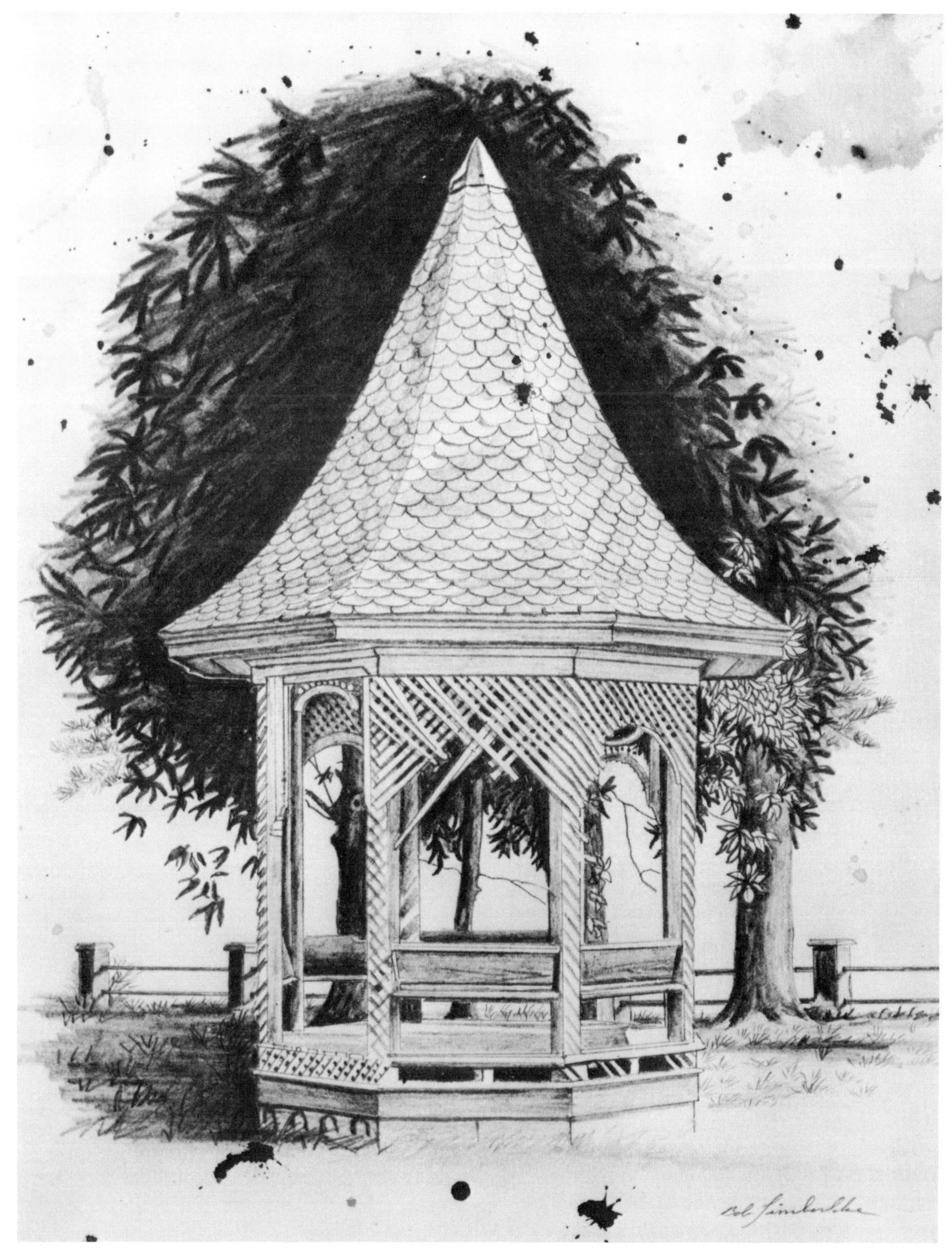

45. Grubb's Gazebo   1978
    Watercolor   30 x 22¼
    Inscribed lower right: Bob Timberlake
    Lent by Mr. and Mrs. Robert L. Grubb

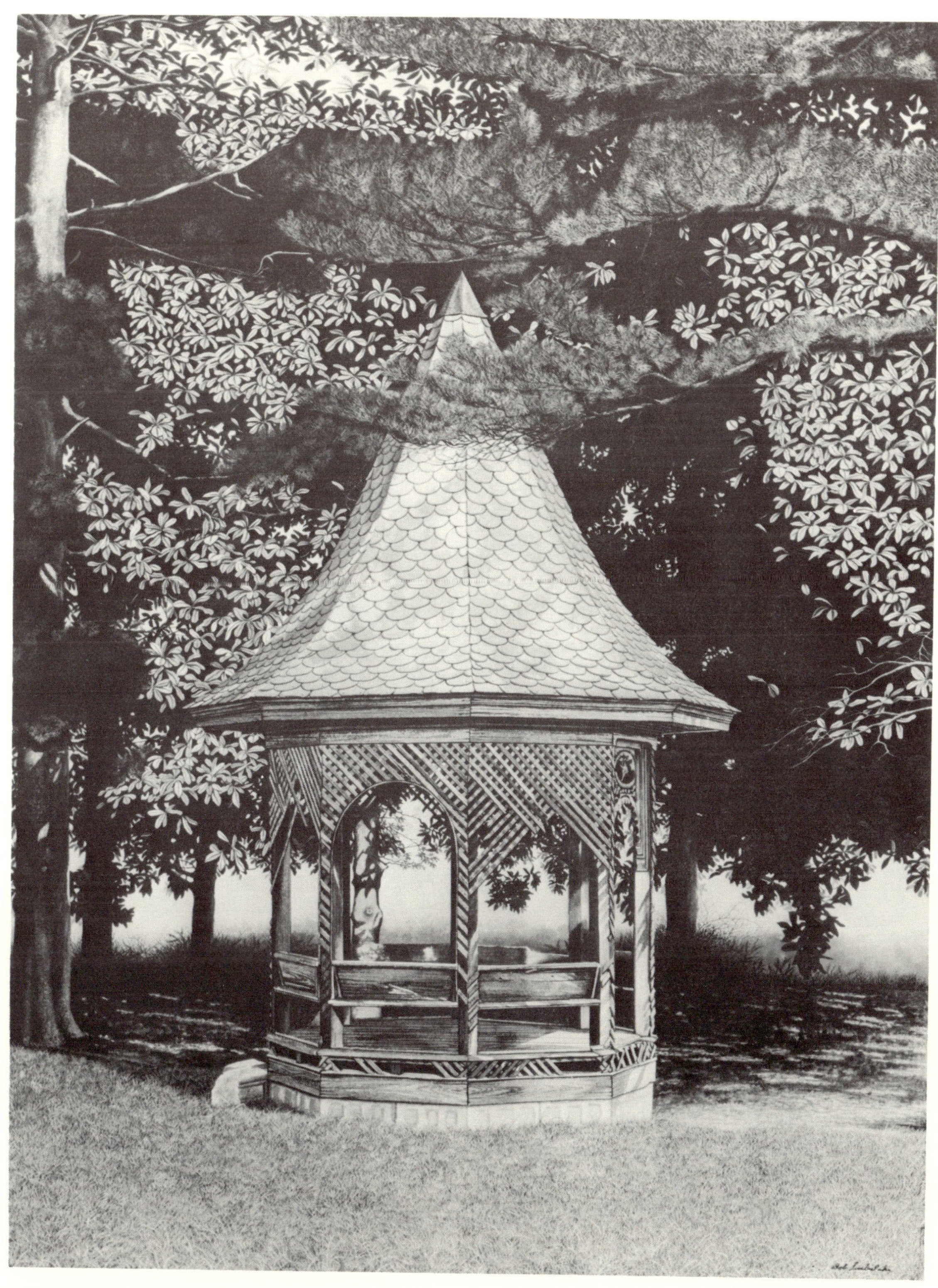

46. Fall Pumpkins   1978
    Watercolor   22 x 15½
    Inscribed upper right: Bob Timberlake
    Lent by Mr. and Mrs. Bob Timberlake

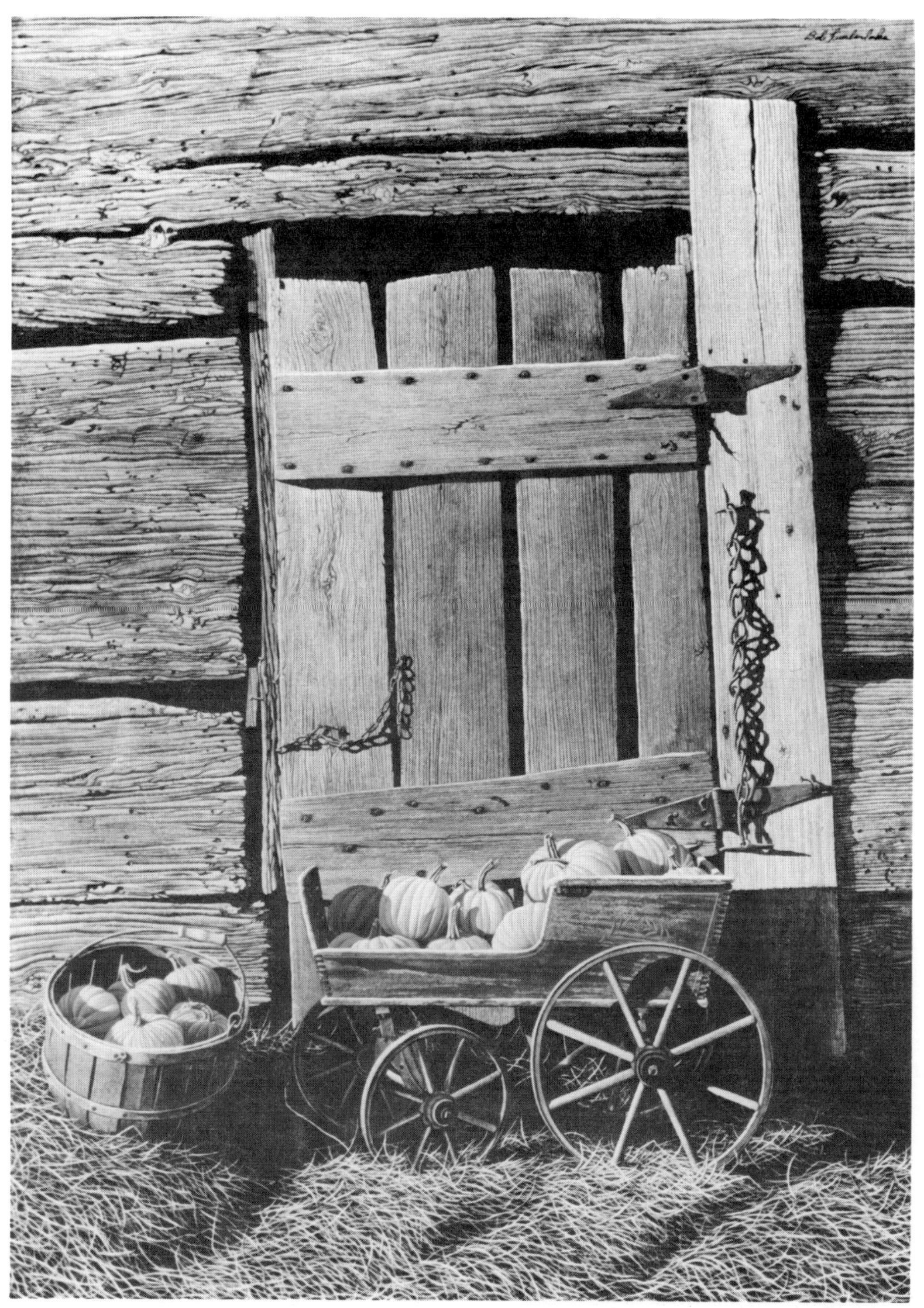

47. Near Grandfather   1978
    Watercolor   18 x 30
    Inscribed lower right: Bob Timberlake
    Private Collection

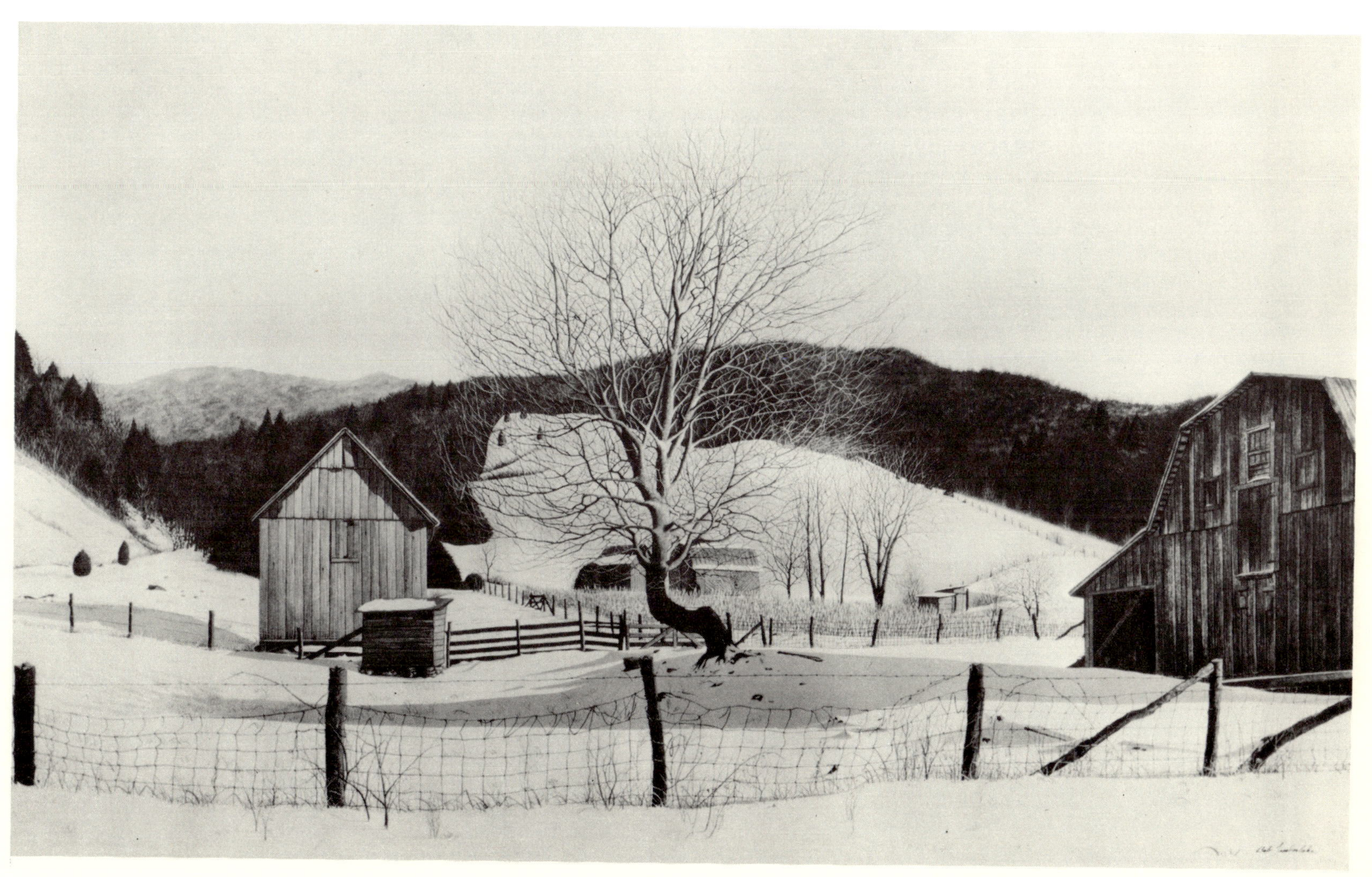

Design: Elaine Sarao Beemer
Printing: Theo Davis Sons, Inc., Zebulon, N. C.